NARA

A CULTURAL GUIDE
to Japan's Ancient Capital

奈良

NARA

A CULTURAL GUIDE
to Japan's Ancient Capital

John H. and Phyllis G. Martin

CHARLES E. TUTTLE COMPANY
Rutland, Vermont & Tokyo, Japan

The publishers would like to acknowledge the cooperation of
Tokyo Kanko Bussan Center for Nara Prefecture

Photographs were taken by the authors

Published by the Charles E. Tuttle Company, Inc.
of Rutland, Vermont & Tokyo, Japan
with editorial offices at
2-6 Suido 1-chome, Bunkyo-ku, Tokyo 112

© 1993 by Charles E. Tuttle Publishing Co., Inc.

LCC Card No. 93-60526
ISBN 0-8048-1914-9

First edition, 1993

Printed in Japan

Contents

TOUR 3: Kofuku-ji and Kasuga Grand Shrine

TOUR 4: **Yakushi-ji, Toshodai-ji, and Daian-ji**

TOUR 5: **Heijo Palace, Hokke-ji, Futai-ji, Kombu-in, and Hannya-ji**

TOUR 6: **Shin Yakushi-ji, Gango-ji, Jurin-ji, and Byakugo-ji**

TOUR 7: **Saidai-ji, Akishino-dera, and Joruri-ji**

TOUR 8: **Horyu-ji, Chugu-ji, and Horin-ji**

ILLUSTRATIONS

MAPS

Introduction
Nara and Its Heritage

J APAN HAD never before seen such splendor. Out of flat farmland at the head of the Yamato Plain, a glorious city had risen almost overnight. It had all the proper aspects required by Chinese geomancy, a science which the Japanese imperial court observed: mountains at its back and to either side, and two rivers coursing across its level plain from the northeast (the Saho River) and the northwest (the Akishino River). Joining to form one stream in the southern reaches of the city, these combined rivers flowed into the open valley to the south and so on to Naniwa (Osaka) and to the Inland Sea. What nature had endowed at the northern end of the Yamato Plain, man would enrich and improve.

Although the Emperor Mommu, just before his early death in 707 in the previous capital of Fujiwara-kyo, had set in motion the plans for a new imperial capital for Japan, it was his father-in-law and his son, two remarkable men, who would ultimately bring the proposed new city to fruition. Fujiwara-no-Fuhito, his father-in-law, was the political leader whose abilities and authority would see to the creation of Heijo-kyo (Citadel of Peace), as Nara was known in its early days. Head of the important Fujiwara clan, he served as first minister to the Japanese rulers who sat upon the throne during his long political incumbency which ended only with his death in 722. He intermarried his daughters into the imperial family, and one such daughter became the wife of Emperor Mommu. At the death of Mommu at age twenty-six in 707, Fuhito's grandson thus became the heir to the throne, a throne to which the youngster would succeed when he came of age.

Under Japanese custom, the future emperor was brought up in his grandfather's mansion where he received the finest of Chinese classical education under the most learned scholars of the day; thus, Fuhito was in charge of the youth's upbringing. When the young man was fourteen, he was married to Fuhito's daughter (a child by Fuhito's second marriage). As a result, Fuhito not only molded the educational and personal development of his grandson, the next-in-line to the throne, but he also provided him with his daughter as a spouse so that their children would have imperial blood as well as Fujiwara blood in their veins. Serving as advisor to the Empress Regent in the interim, Fuhito was responsible for enacting the great Taiho law code which was to govern Japan for years to come. He was responsible, as well, for the development of the new capital of Heijo-kyo and the running of the many departments of state. What was achieved by Fuhito was in time enhanced by his grandson, the Emperor Shomu, when he came to the throne. Between them they brought into being a city of splendid mansions and noble temples and shrines.

Heijo-kyo was based on the plan of the great Chinese capital of Ch'ang-an (present-day Sian), its broad boulevards crossing wide avenues at ninety-degree angles, thereby creating an orderly checkerboard city plan. A great boulevard, the Suzaku-oji (Red Sparrow Boulevard) eighty-four meters (277 feet) wide led from the entry gate to the capital at the southern perimeter of the city to the grand, walled palace compound with its brilliant vermilion gateways at the northern end of this main imperial way.

From the hillside to the east of the city, one looked down on broad boulevards and wide avenues lined with willow trees. The thatch-roofed houses of commoners lay along the lanes behind the boulevards, the board-roofed mansions of the nobility stood out along the major streets, while the tiled roofs of the ceremonial buildings of the court and of the temples shone in the light of the sun. Some fifty pagodas pierced the sky. Noblemen in their silken, colored kimono, priests in their plain black robes, commoners in their simple clothes, and workmen in their scanty loincloths peopled the streets, as did exotically costumed foreigners from abroad.

If Fujiwara-no-Fuhito had brought the city into being, it was his grandson, the pious Emperor Shomu, who would enhance it with splendid temples and glorious images from the Buddhist pantheon of deities. As a young prince and early monarch, Shomu was devoted to a life of pleasure in which hunting occupied many of his hours. In 737, however, smallpox, unintentionally brought by ships from China, swept through Japan, and Shomu became a changed man as the plague decimated the population. Under Chinese lore, evil befell a people when its ruler was at fault, and thus Shomu took this adage to heart, seeking to discover the flaw in his own character which had led to the calamity besetting the nation.

The emperor turned to Buddhism in his search for an answer, and he became a pious Buddhist and a dedicated religious ruler. He saw the Buddha as the protector of the state and its people, and he came to the realization that the teachings of the Buddha offered a guide not only for life in this existence but to the future lives of individuals in their next existence. He was determined to turn Japan into a Buddhist nation, and he began by decreeing that a Buddhist temple and Buddhist sutras be established at the heart of each Japanese provincial capital.

He and his pious consort, the Empress Komyo, dotted Heijo-kyo with temples, monasteries, and nunneries which were meant to be filled with dedicated monks and nuns. The Empress Komyo saw to the building of orphanages, to the creation of centers where medical care could be obtained by the poor, and to houses of refuge for the sick and the elderly. She not only ordered the building of such houses of mercy, but she herself washed the ill and elderly in the hospice belonging to the nunnery to which she eventually retired. Between them, Shomu and Komyo endowed Heijo-kyo with impressive temples filled with splendid images and where colorful ceremonies brought a new richness to the religious life of their time. It was fitting that they took religious orders as a monk and as a nun in the last years of their lives, laying down their imperial power the better to serve the Buddha.

The glory of Heijo-kyo in its great days lasted but three score and ten years. What had come into being in 710 as a glorious capital, meant to last forever, was abandoned by a future emperor in 784. This spurning of Heijo-kyo as the capital was the result of the inept rule of the Empress Koken/Shotoku (she ascended the throne twice), Shomu and Komyo's only child. During her reign, some of the leading Buddhist clergy became more interested in political power than piety, and they thus disturbed the harmony of the state, a harmony called for by Confucian precepts. The empress herself, to the detriment of proper governance, became more enamored of one Buddhist monk than of her imperial duties. Interference in matters political by the clergy led an eventual successor to the empress to abandon Nara and to move the capital to the north, leaving the temples and their clergy behind.

Nara and its religious edifices survived despite the departure of the capital and court as well as the destruction levied by future wars, fires, and earthquakes. Temples and shrines remained, and these noble structures of ancient Nara still stand and continue to retain their magnificent sculptures from earlier centuries, albeit many such buildings are replacements of the original units. Thus present-day Nara, the heir to Heijo-kyo, still enjoys much of the splendor which once graced the northern portion of the historic Yamato Plain. Palaces of emperors and mansions of the aristocracy may be gone, but Nara with its parks, its woodlands, its temples, and its shrines retains a fascinating link with its 1,300 years of history.

Today Nara is a modern city which has filled the space between its eastern and western mountains and has spilled ever further into the plain to the south. It is a contemporary metropolis which maintains the heritage of its past while affording the conveniences of present-day living.

Nara is a city to be enjoyed at leisure. A stay of a few days in one of its hotels or *ryokan* (Japanese-style inns) will provide time for a thorough exploration of a fascinating city little known to Western visitors. There are, of course, one-day tours to Nara from Kyoto and Osaka, but these commercial ventures spend much of their time on the highway or at lunch, thereby offering little more than a tantalizing glimpse of the city's charms.

Contemporary hotels and traditional *ryokan,* as well as a hillside spa, offer comfortable accommodations, while everything from fine cuisine (Japanese and Western) to fast foods is available. Small shops selling Nara specialties, such as traditional calligraphy brushes and ink stones, vie with the latest in a modern department store with its marble halls and its panoramic view over the city from its roof garden. The Kintetsu Line provides speedy access to Osaka or Kyoto, and efficient local bus and taxi services provide connections within Nara as well as to the interesting hinterlands surrounding it.

The political glory may have departed from Nara, but its architectural and artistic grandeur remain to be enjoyed and savored by those fortunate enough to encounter this treasure of early Japanese culture. The founders of the city aptly named it Heijo-kyo, "Citadel of Peace," and so it remains today in the face of the obvious modernization that has occurred. Despite its modern means of transportation and contemporary buildings, Nara still retains the calm and peaceful quality which its temples, shrines, and parks were meant to preserve in the midst of a transient life.

Note: The Japanese characters on half-title pages refer to temples and sights in the chapter. They are read from top to bottom, and from right to left.

TOUR

1

Along Noborioji

登大路

A VISITOR to Nara, having heard of the glories of its temples and shrines, may be somewhat surprised on emerging from either of the railway stations on arrival in this ancient city. Modern stores, comparatively tall buildings, and the flow of traffic are the first images one receives. But one must remember that this is the present day, not the eighth century when Nara was founded. Time does not stand still. Nonetheless, despite all this modernity, the great temples, the colorful shrines, and the tame deer in Nara Park are but a few streets from either the Japan Rail or the Kintetsu Line stations. The modern aspects of present-day Nara life are but a foil for the traditional sites awaiting exploration.

Assuming that one has arrived on a Kintetsu Line train from either Kyoto or Osaka (the quickest way to Nara), one surfaces from the underground station on to Noborioji, the main east-west street of contemporary Nara. (The visitor who uses the JR Line will arrive one long street south of Noborioji.) If ever a street were central to a city, Noborioji with its stores and traffic can serve as a model of a major metropolitan thoroughfare. What a variety this street offers—from the narrow, alley-like streets leading off it at right angles with their small shops and bustling life, to the verdant hills and park at its far end, to its museums and temples on either side of its passage through central Nara. Just a few steps from the Kintetsu Station exit on the south side of Noborioji is Higashi-muki-dori, an arcaded passageway of china shops, traditional *ryokan*, restaurants, antique shops, and even a Christian church. A few more steps to the west from the station exit is the bus station, the taxi concourse, and additional shops, restaurants, banks, and travel agencies.

These shops and restaurants may provide the visitor with those services which can prove helpful, but that is not why one comes to this town. Nonetheless, Noborioji will not disappoint one. By heading east along the south side of the avenue, within two streets the park around the ancient Kofuku-ji temple appears on the right, the Nara National Museum with its treasures of early

Japanese sculpture lies but a little further along the way, and a continuation of one's stroll will lead to the Kasuga Grand Shrine approached by the thousands of lanterns along its tree-shaded path.

If one follows Noborioji to the east on its northern side, the modern Nara Prefectural Office with its art museum and library are but one street along the way. Beyond these attractive modern buildings lie the Neiraku Museum of Ancient Art and the Isui-en Garden, and then the complex of temples which form the Todai-ji with its Great Buddha is at hand, a primary goal of visitors and pilgrims alike.

Perhaps the most interesting way to obtain a sense of Nara, its history, and its traditions can be arrived at before one even leaves the modern high-rise building which sits atop the Kintetsu Line Nara Station, for above the train platforms is a six-story building which houses not only a branch of the famed Nara Hotel but also an exhibition of Nara life and history which is too little known by foreign visitors, the Nara Rekishi Kyoshitsu (Nara Exhibition Hall of Japanese History).

NARA EXHIBITION HALL OF JAPANESE HISTORY

This hall is seldom brought to the attention of foreign visitors since the labels and audio-visual units of its exhibits are all in Japanese. A somewhat sketchy English guide is available, but the exhibits of various aspects of early Japanese life in Nara can be appreciated despite the language barrier.

There is an advantage to the foreign visitor which the designers of the exhibits did not realize: since this museum of early Japan is aimed primarily at schoolchildren, the exhibits are simple enough that a non-Japanese adult can comprehend them. An introduction to Japanese life and history from prehistoric times to the Japanese middle ages is here presented through models, photographs, maps, artifacts, and audio-visual displays. Cutaway models of a pagoda and of traditional farmhouses provide an insight into architectural techniques and living conditions of the past. Reproductions of the Twelve Divine Generals who surround the Yakushi Buddha in the Shin Yakushi-ji temple at the eastern edge of Nara provide an example of the sculptural skill of early Japanese artists.

While classes of Japanese children may throng the exhibits at times, their stay is usually brief, leaving the visitor undisturbed to learn about Japan and living conditions in the Nara area in earlier years. In time, however, when one becomes saturated with knowledge, it is always possible to take a break in the restaurant of the branch of the Nara Hotel in the same building or in one of the restaurants in the fascinating arcaded passageway at street level to the right along Higashi-muki-dori.

NARA PREFECTURAL OFFICES AND MUSEUM

Crossing to the north side of Noborioji and walking to the east, one soon passes one of the most attractive shops in Nara, a shop which specializes in fine articles of Japanese arts and crafts. Beyond the shops, the architecturally contemporary offices of Nara Prefecture are next along the avenue. The prefecture did not always boast such magnificent buildings. In the 1870s when the Meiji-era government came into power, its leaders had a decidedly anti-Buddhist attitude, and many temples suffered from their dislike of Buddhism and their favoring of Shinto as a virtual state religion. One of the temples which suffered was the Kofuku-ji across Noborioji. Much of its land was alienated from it, and even some of its buildings were seized to house the offices of the new prefectural government.

In time, under more enlightened government and the growth of prefectural office needs, the government moved out of the temple structures, and in the 1960s a modern prefectural complex was created to house the prefectural offices, the prefectural court, the prefectural library, and the prefectural art museum. In an unusual blend of past and modern architectural styles, elements of contemporary and traditional architecture were combined in the use of the post-and-beam idiom and in the building rooflines which reflect past architectural forms. Thus the complex provides a striking and attractive official center for the prefecture.

The unit of these governmental buildings which is of most interest to the visitor is the Nara Prefectural Art Museum. Located just behind the main prefectural buildings, to the north of Noborioji, the museum mounts a number of exhibitions each year. Such exhibitions come either from the museum's collections of ceramics and woodblock prints or from materials borrowed from other museums or private collections. The museum is always worthy of a visit.

NEIRAKU MUSEUM
One short street beyond the prefectural offices and the major north-south street at the eastern side of the office, a side street

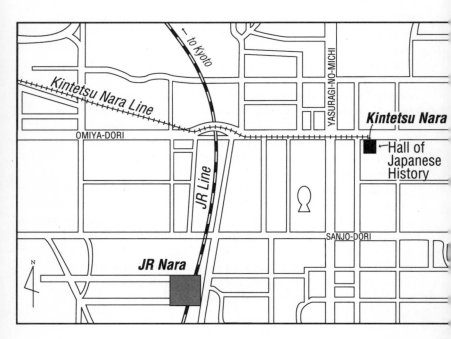

turns to the left and then to the right, leaving one before the private Neiraku Museum and Isui-en Garden. The museum houses a collection of more than two thousand art objects from China, Korea, and Japan from early times. Only a portion of this excellent collection of Chinese bronzes of the Yin and Chou dynasties, mirrors from the Warring States times, and ceramics from all three countries is on view at any one time in the one-story museum building, and the exhibits are always a delight to the connoisseur of early Asian art. In addition, a special exhibition is mounted in the museum each year from April 1 to the following March 20.

ISUI-EN GARDEN

Of more interest to the average visitor is the adjacent Isui-en Garden which provides a delightful, traditional Japanese stroll

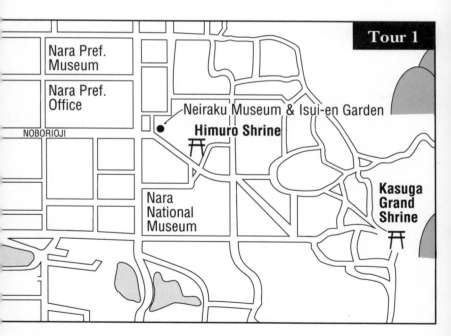

garden of the Meiji period (1868–1912) just a short distance from busy Noborioji. The gentle Yoshiki River, more a brook than a river, meanders through the garden, through wooded glades, past azalea bushes, cherry, plum, and maple trees—whose springtime flowers or autumnal colors enhance the beauty of the garden. Stone lanterns, stone water basins, small tea houses with thatched or cryptomeria bark roofs add to the ambience of this lovely garden. The pleasures of the garden can be further enhanced if one makes reservations beforehand for a tea-ceremony service in one of the attractive traditional tea houses in the garden or for a *kaiseki* (Japanese high cuisine) lunch. The loveliness of the garden is enhanced by the "borrowed scenery" the designer had in mind when making his plans—of the slopes of Wakakusayama (Mt. Wakakusa), Mt. Kasuga, and the huge roof of the Todai-ji's Great Buddha Hall which provide a backdrop to the garden.

NARA NATIONAL MUSEUM

One street further east on Noborioji and diagonally across from the prefectural complex are the Nara National Museum's two buildings in a portion of what was once a part of the Kofuku-ji temple grounds and which has now, in essence, become the beginning of the open parkland of Nara Park. The museum had its start in the period after 1870 when, under pressure, many temples had to surrender a number of their prize objects to the government. National museums were thus created in Tokyo and Kyoto in the 1870s, and then in 1898 a museum building in the European beaux-arts architectural style was constructed in Nara to hold the art being gathered in the area. In 1973 a modern building, primarily created for large special exhibitions, was built behind the original Nara National Museum. This modern facility is in the traditional *azekura* (log-cabin style) of architecture which is reminiscent of the ancient treasure houses of Japanese temples. The style is ancient, but the modern facilities and the poured concrete construction provide a treasure house which is fireproof and, it is hoped, earthquake proof. It and its predecessor are connected by an underground tunnel.

The Nara National Museum concentrates primarily on the art of Japan from the period just prior to A.D. 600, when Chinese influence awakened Japanese artistic capabilities, through to the flowering of Japanese art in the Middle Ages. The beaux-arts building houses the permanent collection, much of it, as indicated above, from temples in Nara Prefecture while the new building is primarily used for interesting temporary exhibitions.

The most notable exhibition each year in the new building is the annual display of a selection of the treasures from the Shoso-in, the treasury of the Todai-ji temple. These treasures were once the personal belongings of the Emperor Shomu who died in 756, and they represent the arts and crafts of the known world of his day. The objects range from glass from Persia to the arts of India, Central Asia, and China. These selections are normally on view from October 20 to November 6, and they should not be missed. In addition, there is also a special exhibition of traditional Japanese art which opens each May.

Behind the 1898 museum building is a large image of the Buddha such as was sculpted from the rock hills near Usuki, Kyushu, while just to the south of the newer museum building is the Hasso-in, a small, rustic tea house in the Furuta Oribe style. The tea house may be visited upon request at the museum office.

HIMURO SHRINE

The primary Shinto shrine in Nara is the Kasuga Grand Shrine, one of those sites which is a must on anyone's list of places to visit in Nara. It is a rich and tradition-laden shrine of the Fujiwara family who for centuries were the ruling political force behind the throne. As such it is historically fascinating; in its richness of style and ceremonial events, however, it is quite atypical of the traditional common-people's Shinto shrine.

More representative of the many neighborhood Shinto places of worship throughout Japan is the Himuro Shrine, a small

Shinto shrine which is across Noborioji from the newer Nara National Museum building. Small and unimportant as it is, it is worthy of a visit in contrast to the ostentation of the Kasuga Grand Shrine.

A torii stands at the entrance to the Himuro Shrine which is enclosed on three sides by its Kairo, a roofed-corridor structure. A stage-like Haiden (offertory) is in the center of the enclosed area, and here religious services, offerings to the deity, or religious dances or ceremonies can take place to please the gods. The Haiden stands in front of the main structure of the shrine, the Honden (spirit hall), in which the local kami (spirit or god) is enshrined. All is quite simple, as is normal with small Shinto shrines. The one touch of splendor can sometimes be seen along the sides of the corridors—the modern shrine festival cart, a replica of an early Japanese oxen-drawn vehicle, which is stored between shrine festivals in its component parts under the protecting roof of the shrine corridors.

Beyond the Himuro Shrine, Noborioji at the next crossroad leads to the pathway on the left which heads into the Todai-ji temple grounds. The entryway cannot be missed since it is always crowded with visitors to the Todai-ji, and the path is easily recognized by the many souvenir stalls on its western side. The temple is the main attraction of visitors to Nara, and thus it is worthy of a tour of its own—as is described in Tour 2.

TOUR

2

WHEN IN 745 the pious Emperor Shomu decreed the construction of the Todai-ji, the Great Eastern Temple, he determined that Japan would have the largest bronze image of the Buddha which would be housed in the greatest wooden building in the world. Seldom has such vaulting ambition been so well realized—for the Great Buddha Hall, the Daibutsuden, still stands and can still claim to be the largest wooden building containing the largest bronze image in the world. It can continue to make this claim despite the fact that disasters have seen both the image and the building destroyed and then re-created more than once. Of course, the hall is now but two-thirds its original size and the Buddha is some five feet smaller than the image of Emperor Shomu's time, but the two units are still most impressive and the pride of Nara.

Fearful that he might die before his dream was completely realized, the ailing Emperor Shomu had the Great Buddha dedicated in 752 before its covering of gold leaf had been applied. There hadn't been gold enough in Japan to gild so huge an image, but then, almost miraculously, gold had been found in the Province of Mutsu. Taking this discovery as a divine blessing, the emperor had led his court before the as yet unfinished Buddha image, and in a religious service, this descendent of the Shinto gods here proclaimed himself the humble servant of the Buddha. Today, the present image, once more without its golden sheen, appears to current visitors or pilgrims much as the emperor would have seen it more than 1,200 years ago at the time of its dedication since past fires have removed the gold leaf which was applied shortly after the emperor's death.

So great a religious undertaking deserved an appropriately glorious dedication. Therefore some ten thousand Buddhist monks were gathered in 752 in the forecourt of the Great Buddha Hall while distinguished priests led the rhythmic chanting of solemn praises of the Buddha. Colorful pennants about the hall flapped in the breeze outside the towering building as the important Indian Buddhist priest Bodhisena painted in the eyes of the Great Buddha image within. Cords were attached to the brush Bodhisena wielded, its ends held in the hands of Emperor Shomu and his gentle Empress Komyo so they could partake of the momentous Eye Opening Ceremony which would symbolically bring the great image to life.

The ten thousand monks and other distinguished guests who were present on that solemn occasion have long since passed on to other Buddhist reincarnations or to nirvana. Today they are replaced by the thousands who throng the lane leading from Noborioji, visitors who patronize the souvenir stalls along the way, or stop to watch the tame deer who are ever eager for the handout of wafers which giggling Japanese schoolgirls timidly offer them. The path leads on to the massive gateway which provides the main entry to the Todai-ji grounds.

MAIN BUILDINGS OF TODAI-JI

NANDAI-MON

Beyond the souvenir stalls lies the Great South Gate, the Nandai-mon, which separates the realm of everyday life from the area where the law of the Buddha has been proclaimed for thirteen centuries. The huge 62.3-foot-high Nandai-mon from 1199, created in an Indian architectural style, is but two-thirds the size of the original gateway which was leveled by a typhoon in 962, but it still provides an awe-inspiring entrance to the temple grounds.

The gigantic structure has five bays, the central three units being passageways while the end bays hold the magnificent statues of the Benevolent Kings who guard the temple against malevolent forces. With their scowling faces and their threatening stance they may not appear to be benevolent, but their anger is aimed only against evildoers—and so we can fearlessly pass by these twenty-five-foot guardians of Buddhist truths. These tremendous wooden Nio images are attributed to two of the leading sculptors of the late twelfth and early thirteenth century, Unkei and Kaikei, both members of the distinguished Kei family of sculptors who were influenced by the artistry of Sung dynasty China. Behind the Benevolent Kings, facing toward the lane which continues to the Great Buddha Hall, are two six-foot-tall stone *koma-inu*, traditional lion-dogs who also serve as guardians, created by a Chinese artist in 1196 at the time of the construction of the present gate. They offer additional protection to the Todai-ji.

HONBO

Ahead on the left lie the buildings of the temple's junior and senior high schools, education always having been a primary concern of Japanese Buddhism. To the right is the Honbo, the temple office, with its small treasury whose holdings include the famous Birthday Buddha of 752, a small bronze image of the newborn, historic Buddha standing in a bronze bowl. One hand is raised toward heaven while the other hand points to earth to indicate his dominion over both realms.

FORMER PAGODAS

At one time the Great Buddha Hall was preceded by two huge pagodas which soared 328 feet above the temple complex. Topped by metal *sorin* (spires), these units unfortunately acted as lightning rods, and so both pagodas were consumed by fire during thunderstorms in their early years. Today the broad base of the Sai-to (West Pagoda) and the To-to (East Pagoda) can still be discerned some five hundred feet to the west and east of the main path to the Buddha Hall. Closer to the path on the right is the Kagami-ike, the Mirror Pond. A small, vermilion, Shinto shrine on an island in the midst of the pond offers the protection of the native Shinto gods to the Buddha and his bodhisattvas in the Great Buddha Hall.

KAIRO AND CHU-MON

The path ends at the Kairo (corridor) which surrounds the Buddha Hall. In the center of the Kairo is the Chu-mon (Central

Gateway) which both terminates the path and at the same time offers a view of the huge Daibutsuden (Great Buddha Hall) beyond this gate. As with the Nandai-mon, here a forbidding-looking Guardian King in either side bay of the Chu-mon protects the inner temple complex from evil spirits. The Chu-mon is only opened upon ceremonial occasions, and thus a turn to the left brings one to the entry to the inner grounds of the Great Buddha Hall at the far end of the front corridor. The ticket counter is inside the entry at this western end of the Kairo.

GREAT LANTERN

The three arms of the Kairo encircle a courtyard before the Great Buddha Hall. A central pathway leads from the medium-sized incense pot in the middle of the south corridor wing (just inside the Chu-mon) to the very large, roofed incense pot at the top of the entry steps to the Buddha Hall at the end of this inner path. Three-fourths of the way along the path stands the noted 14.7-foot-tall octagonal bronze lantern of 752, its eight panels enriched with diamond-patterned metal lattice work. Four of the panels display Korean lion-dogs while the other four panels show heavenly beings playing musical instruments. Some see these figures as bodhisattvas, Buddhist saints (to use a Western phrase) who have been among the favorite Buddhist deities through the centuries in Japan. They are beings who through their perfection can attain Enlightment but who have refrained from entering nirvana in order to help others toward that more blessed state. Here these graceful images offer an aspect of the visual appeal which art brought to religion in the eighth century, as well as the *joie de vivre* of that period.

Atop the lantern is a *centamani,* a flaming jewel, a miraculous treasure which can grant the fulfillment of wishes, a jewel often held in the hand of Buddhist images of Jizo, the protector of children, and of some Kannon images, the Bodhisattva of Mercy. To the right of the lantern is a roofed ablution fountain where worshippers may cleanse and purify themselves before entering the hall straight ahead. Visitors can be seen to rinse their mouths (of impure thoughts and words) and their hands (of impure actions) before continuing to the innermost portion of the temple.

BINZURU

The Daibutsuden provides an overwhelming sensation as one mounts the steps before this gigantic wooden structure. A large, roofed incense pot stands atop the steps, and here worshippers place incense sticks in the sand in the pot and say a prayer before

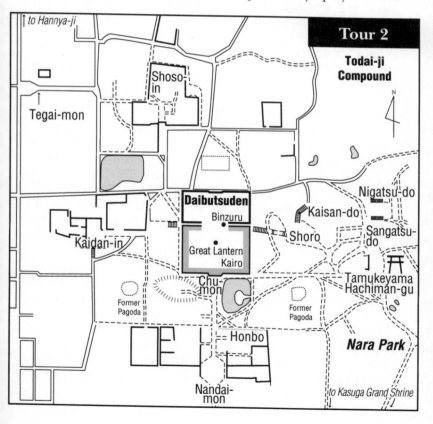

entering the building. Elderly women in their formal kimono, hands clasped in prayer as the smoke of the incense rises about them, make a charming scene.

Less charming but nonetheless intriguing is the over-sized image of Binzuru who is seated on the outside veranda of the Daibutsuden to the right of the huge entry doors to the hall. Ensconced on a wooden Chinese chair, he sits impassively under his red cap and his red bib, gazing on the throngs before him. A disciple of the Buddha when Gautama was still in this world, Binzuru must always remain outside temple buildings because of moral shortcomings during his lifetime. (Was it alcohol or women or some other deviation from the Buddha's teachings which led to his fall from grace? Tradition differs about his failings.) A folk belief holds that the touching of Binzuru (who was a physician by profession) and then the touching of an afflicted area of one's body can result in a cure for illness.

DAIBUTSUDEN AND DAIBUTSU

To say that the Daibutsuden is overwhelming is to put it mildly. Some 188 feet long by 165 feet wide and reaching 166 feet into the sky, the present wooden structure was created in 1709 to replace the one which had burned down decades earlier. Within is the Daibutsu, the Great Buddha, rising 48.5 feet tall, just five feet shorter than the image the Emperor Shomu reverenced. This gigantic Vairocana Buddha (Birushana Butsu in Japanese) is the Buddha of Illumination and of the Sun, the Cosmic Buddha whose spirit manifests itself in the many Buddhas and bodhisattvas who partake of his spirit in their goal of saving all sentient beings. The image dominates the huge hall built to house it, as it was meant to dominate the life of the Japanese to help to bring them to the Buddha's truths.

When the plans for the Daibutsuden and its Daibutsu were being made, the Emperor Shomu worried whether the ancient Japanese gods of the Shinto faith might be offended by this project in favor of Buddhism. Thus he sent one of his trusted priests, Gyogi, to the most sacred Shinto shrine at Ise to ask the Sun Goddess Amaterasu (the heavenly ancestor of the imperial family and progenitor of the emperor) whether the project found favor with the Shinto deities. The goddess, according to tradition, spoke in Chinese to the suppliant priest in a dream, saying that the Buddha and the sun were one. The way was clear for the project to proceed.

Within the huge hall, seated on a high podium which is surrounded by inscribed bronze lotus leaves and with an altar before him, the Vairocana Buddha gazes beneficently on worshippers below. A huge golden aureole rises behind the Buddha, sixteen small Buddhas standing out against its golden background. The position (mudra) of the fingers and hands of the main image have religious significance. That of the right hand indicates the granting of ease of mind while the mudra of the left hand signifies the granting of wishes. The upturned hand is so large (6.5 feet) that five monks can stand in the Buddha's palm while dusting the figure.

Never before had so huge a metal image been cast. Workmen were drafted from all the provinces to work on the project, and a huge mound was built about the form into which the liquid bronze would be poured to create the Buddha. As each pouring progressed, the mound with its molds rose higher so that the next level could be cast. When the metal had cooled, the mound was leveled and the forms removed, the Buddha appearing in all his glory to await the gilding by craftsmen. Many of these craftsmen involved in the gilding process sickened and died as the gilding went on, victims of an unknown disease. Today we know that they died of mercury poisoning from the amalgam in which the gold was held.

The Buddha in many temples in Japan is not alone in his glory, for he is usually accompanied by assisting bodhisattvas to form a triad at the center of the temple. Here in the Daibutsuden, on the Buddha's left is the Bodhisattva Nyorin Kannon who answers prayers and grants good fortune through the *centamani* jewel in his hand. On the left is the image of Kokuzo who possesses wisdom and happiness as vast as the air about us. Normally the main images are protected by the Shitenno, the Four Guardian Kings. Here but two remain, one on each side of the Buddha: Komoku-ten, Guardian of the West, on the Buddha's left while Tamoku-ten, Guardian of the North, is on the right. Both kings stand on squirming demons which they are righteously stamping out of existence.

At the rear left of the building is a model of the Todai-ji complex prior to its initial destruction in the 1100s. The model provides an excellent overview of the original shape of the temple, even though the pagodas are misplaced in the model since they stood before the complex instead of beside it. At the rear right of the building are artifacts from the temple's past, and these include the huge heads of one-time images of the temple as well as the curved *shibi* (owls' tails) from the ends of the roof—charms meant to ward off lightning and fire.

In front of these reminders of the past is an enormous pillar with a square hole at its base. This innocuous-looking unit is the cause of much mirth to Japanese visitors. Tradition claims that if one can wriggle through this narrow opening, one is assured of entry into the Buddha's heaven. Thus friends can be seen cheering on their companions who are trying mightily to squeeze through the restricted space. Plump individuals obviously will never attain paradise!

KAIDAN-IN

The Emperor Shomu was concerned that Buddhism in Japan be fully grounded in the Buddhist heritage and reflect the highest forms and ideals of the faith. He therefore invited the noted Chinese Buddhist monk Ganjin to come to Japan to set up his Kaidan, or ordination platform, so as to properly ordain priests who had previously lacked such religious affirmation. The emperor desired Ganjin to reform Japanese Buddhism as well so as to make it conform fully to the finest practices of Buddhism.

Ganjin had made numerous unsuccessful attempts to reach Japan, and on his sixth voyage he at last arrived in the island kingdom. Previously attempted journeys had resulted in ship-wreck and had caused saltwater damage to his eyes, injuries which had led to his becoming blind. Soon after his arrival in Nara in 753, after the dedication of the Daibutsu, Ganjin set up his ordination platform in front of the Daibutsuden on earth he had brought with him from the sacred Mt. Wu Tai Shan in China. On this platform in a solemn ceremony he ordained not only those monks worthy of ordination, but also the retired Emperor Shomu, the Dowager Empress Komyo, and their daughter, the reigning Empress Koken. Dissatisfied in time with the attitudes and religious commitment of the monks at the Todai-ji, monks who seemed too interested in political power and private ad-vancement, Ganjin moved his Kaidan to the Toshodai-ji in southwestern Nara in 759, a new monastery he was permitted to establish by Shomu's successor, his daughter the Empress Koken.

An ordination platform remained at the Todai-ji, although it was eventually moved from in front of the Daibutsuden and in time to its present site to the west. For almost a century, the Kaidan (*kai* = precepts, *dan* = platform) at the Todai-ji and at the Toshodai-ji were the only two platforms where Buddhist ordina-tion of priests could take place in Japan. (In 822 the Emperor Saga authorized the construction of an additional Kaidan at the Enryaku-ji temple outside of Kyoto, thereby breaking Nara's monopoly on priestly ordination.)

Within the present Todai-ji Kaidan-in hall of 1731, seven feet above the floor is the raised ordination platform on which monks make their profession. If for no other reason, the building should be visited in order to see the exquisite Shitenno (Four Heavenly Kings), four dry-clay images which stand at each of the four corners of the platform. These delightful polychromed figures are among the finest statuary in Japan, and they show the influence of the advanced artistry of Tang China in the 700s. Each realistic image is life-sized and stands upon a demon it is quelling. The Four Heavenly Kings are:

1. **Komoku-ten:** Guardian of the West, holding a writing brush in one hand and a scroll in the other hand, writing down the shortcomings of sinners against Buddhist truths.
2. **Tamon-ten (Bishamon-ten):** Guardian of the North, a small pagoda resting on his upturned palm in symbolic defense of Buddhism.
3. **Jikoku-ten:** Guardian of the East, drawing his sword in defense of the faith.
4. **Zocho-ten:** Guardian of the South, holding a staff as a symbol of office and as a weapon.

Two twenty-inch-tall images of the Shaka Nyorai Buddha and of the Taho Buddha are seated in a small pagoda in the center of the ordination platform. These images are said to have come from China with Ganjin, although present research dates them to the 750s and considers them to be of Japanese origin.

Behind the Daibutsuden, en route from the Kaidan-in to the Shoso-in, a flat area is encountered with its remains of the stone bases for columns which once held up the roof of the Todai-ji Kodo or lecture hall. Here the monks gathered for instruction while adjacent were the monastic dormitories, all these buildings have long since vanished. The area of the Kodo, with a pond to the west and the huge bulk of the Daibutsuden behind it, is a wonderful place for enjoying a picnic lunch before continuing a further exploration of this major Nara temple.

SHOSO-IN

One of the greatest and most extraordinary treasure houses of the world, the Shoso-in (chief repository) stands to the north of both the Daibutsuden and the site of the former Kodo. This original *azekura* treasury of the Todai-ji was created in the mid-700s, and it is one of the few eighth-century structures not to have been destroyed by earthquakes, fire, or war through the centuries. From 756, on the death of Emperor Shomu, this building became the repository of the ten thousand treasures which had belonged to the emperor and which his grieving Empress Komyo had given to the Todai-ji for the sake of the repose of the emperor's soul.

A wooden building of interlocking cypress logs, it is 108 feet long by 30.8 feet wide and stands 46.7 feet tall. It is raised on forty tall, wooden pillars each three feet in diameter and rising 8.9 feet so as to keep the floor of the structure above the ground. Ostensibly the raised position of the building permitted air to circulate about it in humid periods so as to protect its contents against mold. In like manner, the logs of the walls are purported to swell in damp weather to keep out moisture and then to shrink in dry weather to permit the building to breathe, thus protecting the treasures within. In recent years, however, this theory has been brought into question, but the fact remains that the treasures have been miraculously preserved for more than twelve centuries in this wooden building.

The doors to the Shoso-in have unusual locks: the hasps of the doors are tied with a rope which is then encased in a paper document with the seal of the emperor, written in his own hand. This is then cased with a bamboo cover which is then shielded by a wooden box. The locking or unlocking of the doors may only be done in the presence of an imperial messenger—and so the doors have remained inviolate to unwarranted opening through twelve centuries.

The treasures preserved in the Shoso-in are among the most remarkable in the world. They include musical instruments from Southeast Asia, silver ewers from Persia, glass objects from the Near East, bronze mirrors from China, medicines, and textiles from the then known world, all created before the emperor's death in 756. The wealth of the world from ancient times which traversed the fabled Silk Road and the Asian seas in the mid-700s as gifts to the imperial court here found safekeeping in Japan. All these treasures, other examples of which have disappeared from China and other lands, were preserved in this wooden building through the centuries. Each year in late October and early November visitors may see a selection of these remarkable objects in the Nara National Museum at an annual modern version of the traditional autumn "airing of the treasures."

Since the Second World War, two modern concrete treasuries have been built within the grounds of the Shoso-in complex, the better to protect and to conserve these eighth-century treasures. Thus the original wooden storage building no longer houses the objects given to the Todai-ji in 756. The grounds of the Shoso-in are open at the end of October and early November (when some of the treasures are on view in the National Museum) so that this ancient repository may be seen at close hand.

TEGAI-MON

To the north and west of the Shoso-in, opposite Ichijo-dori (First Avenue) the street which led from the imperial palace to the eastern side of the capital and to the Todai-ji, is the Tegai-mon gate. This impressive entrance to the western sector of the Todai-ji grounds is unusual in that above the portals of this Buddhist temple gate there hangs a huge *shimenawa,* a thick, sacred, Shinto rope. The *shimenawa* dates back to the 750s when the sacred cart bringing the Shinto kami Hachiman arrived in Kyoto from Kyushu from which he was carried by an honorary imperial bodyguard of soldiers and court retainers in order to serve as a Shinto protector to the new Buddhist temple. The new shrine to this Shinto god was not ready for his reception on his arrival, and thus for a number of days the cart rested in the Tegai-mon gate while Buddhist priests chanted prayers before it. In remembrance of this occasion, the Shinto *shimenawa* still hangs above the entrance opening of the gate. The gate had an additional benefit for Nara, if tradition can be believed, since it was held that any disease could be cured by simply walking past the gate.

SUB-TEMPLES OF TODAI-JI

The Emperor Shomu's plans for the Todai-ji were grandiose, to say the least. Not only did he order the construction of the largest Buddha image in the world and the largest wooden hall to encompass it, but he planned for sufficient sub-temples and Shinto shrines so that the Todai-ji would be the envy of the Buddhist world—particularly of China whose capital of Ch'ang-an (Sian) was the model for Nara as the capital of Japan.

Grandiose plans had to be tempered with caution, however, since the government had never before put so much money and effort into enhancing the Buddhist faith, a religion which had only flowered in Japan in the previous one hundred and fifty years. Would the Shinto gods be offended by the development of the Todai-ji? The emperor had taken the precaution of sending an emissary to Ise to ascertain the feelings of the goddess Amaterasu, the progenitor of the imperial line. Her answer had been eminently satisfactory, but might other Shinto gods be offended? There was nothing like another opinion, and thus a second emissary was dispatched to the great Shinto shrine in Usa on the island of Kyushu to determine the attitude of Hachiman, the deity of war. Not only did Hachiman declare that he favored the construction of the Todai-ji and would help in its construction, but he indicated that he would see that the other Shinto deities would concur with his decision.

So delighted was Shomu with this answer that he bestowed a cap of honor on the god, and he sent a detachment of soldiers to accompany Hachiman to Nara in a sacred cart. A shrine was ordered to be constructed for Hachiman on the grounds of the Todai-ji, but the speed of the military detachment was so great that the god and the god cart arrived before the new shrine was ready. In this embarrassing situation, the god cart had to be stationed at the Tegai-mon gate (as explained above), and the Buddhist priests, who chanted continuous prayers about the cart until the shrine was ready, were doing their best at the emperor's urging to assuage any disappointment or second thoughts on the part of Hachiman.

TAMUKEYAMA HACHIMAN-GU

Shinto shrines had served the Japanese people from time immemorial, and they were always simple structures, if structures at all. With the coming of Buddhism to Japan in the late 500s, a change in Shinto shrines began. As Buddhist temples arose in the ornate Chinese style of architecture, some Shinto shrines began to enhance their sites with aspects of Chinese architecture also. Perhaps the most notable aspect of the Hachiman Shrine at the Todai-ji is the ornate, two-story, vermilion gateway, the Ro-mon, which leads into the shrine. This gateway was obviously inspired by the new artistic influences arriving from China, and it befitted a shrine to a major Shinto deity who was to serve as the primary Shinto protector of the new Buddhist monastery and temple of the Todai-ji. The gateway is accompanied by additional rooms to its left and right so that the structure offers an imposing facade to those approaching it.

The Hachiman Shrine is most easily reached from the main entrance to the Todai-ji temple. When one walks through the great Nandai-mon gate to the Chu-mon, the ceremonial gateway to the Daibutsuden complex, a turn to the right and then a walk up the hill through a large vermilion torii brings one to the Hachiman shrine and the other sub-temples on the hillside to the east of the Daibutsuden.

Within the grounds of the Hachiman Shrine, beyond the Ro-mon gateway, is the stage-like roofed Haiden, the offertory, where Shinto priests (since a new priesthood did develop as a simpler counterpart to the highly organized Buddhist priest-hood and hierarchy) could make offerings to Hachiman and the other Shinto gods here enshrined. The Haiden could also be used for entertainment, including sacred dances, since it was important to please the gods with offerings of entertainment as well as food.

Beyond the Haiden, in an area fenced from the public, stands the multi-part shrine unit which houses Hachiman and other Shinto deities, the Sumiyoshi sub-shrine having its own buildings. Often a priest in his white robes and his black *eboshi,* the ancient court hat of the nobility, can be seen making offerings to the gods. In the background is a modern fireproof, concrete treasure house where the treasures of the shrine can be kept in safety.

The concrete treasury has its ancient counterpart in front of the Ro-mon gateway to the Hachiman Shrine. Here are two small log-cabin treasuries in the traditional *azekura* style of architecture. The southern one belongs to the Hachiman Shrine while the northern one is a treasury for the adjacent Sangatsu-do temple. Such treasuries are often an anachronism today, for the Japanese government has been concerned in recent years to assist temples in building fireproof treasuries lest their ancient art objects fall prey to damage from fire, earthquakes, or typhoons.

SANGATSU-DO

To the north of the Hachiman Shrine, this structure has a simple exterior which belies the riches of the treasures which lie within its walls. Called the Sangatsu-do, the Third Month Hall, its name derives from the sutra reading ceremonies held here in the third month of the year under the ancient lunar calendar. Consisting of two joined buildings, the northern unit is important not only because of the early Buddhist images within it, but since it is the oldest structure in the Todai-ji. Since it was first constructed in 733, it even predates the Todai-ji Daibutsuden which was not begun until a dozen years later. Since it held so many sacred objects, a second building, the Raido or worship hall, was added before it in which the priests could chant sutras or worshippers could pray to the images in the inner building. In the 1100s the two were joined under one roof.

One first enters the Raido, the worship hall, where today the entry fee to the Sangatsu-do is paid, and then one moves from this very plain building into the inner building with its amazing collection of early Buddhist images. So rich is the Sangatsu-do in such early figures that a tatami-covered bench has been provided on the south wall of this inner building to permit one to sit in contemplation of these Buddhist deities.

The main image of the Sangatsu-do is an 11.8-foot-tall Fukukensaku Kannon. Kannon has always been a favorite Buddhist deity in Japan, for he is seen as the Bodhisattva of Mercy. This imposing eighth-century figure with eight arms was created with the new dry-lacquer technique, and his head bears a diadem of perforated silver at the front of which is a miniature silver figure of Amida Buddha. Some 20,000 pearls, crystals, agates, and a number of *maga-tama* (comma-shaped jewels) are threaded about his crown. In his hands is the "never empty lasso" (the meaning of Fukukensaku) with which Kannon saves all beings.

On either side of the Kannon stand the Nikko (Sunlight) and Gakko (Moonlight) Bodhisattvas, two of the most noted eighth-century images in Japan. Standing 6.5 feet tall, they have great dignity in their quiet, prayerful, and meditative stance. Four rather crude Shitenno, the Four Guardian or Heavenly Kings, stand at the four corners of the image area guarding the deities between them. It is possible that the original Shitenno were the more attractive guardians which are now in the Kaidan-in and which were transferred from the Sangatsu-do to the Kaidan-in when the latter sub-temple lost its images to a fire. Two Kongo Rikishi, Benevolent Kings, stand in the forefront. As guardians of the holy areas of Buddhism, usually seen in the end bays of temple gateways, their role is to frighten evil away. As a result, their countenances are not among the most inviting.

The additional images consist of a dignified Bon-ten (the Indian god Brahma) and a Taishaku-ten (the Indian god Indra), each thirteen feet tall. At the rear of the image platform is a Kichijo-ten, the deity of wealth, good fortune, and beauty, and a Benzai-ten, the deity of music, good fortune, health, long life, and oratory, each clothed in the style of eighth-century court ladies. These latter two were damaged in an early fire in the former temple in which they once resided. In a cabinet behind the Fukukensaku Kannon is the Shikkongo-shin, a *hibutsu* or hidden image. Such hidden images exist in many temples and are either exhibited but once or twice a year or else are considered so sacred that they cannot even be seen by the priests in the temples which hold them. This colorful image with his scowling face, a spear in his hand ready for action, is shown only on December 16, the day on which Abbot Roben, the founding priest of the Todai-ji, died in 773.

NIGATSU-DO

If the Hachiman Shrine, other than its handsome gateway, is of a rather simple construction, and if the Sangatsu-do is even more unostentatious in its outward appearance, the prize for an impressive structure must go to the Nigatsu-do, the Second Month Hall. Placed upon a hillside, its front portion resting on tall wooden posts, the main hall is reached by either of two separate staircases rising to the respective sides of the hall from the main path below. Of the two staircases, the open-air southern one leads up to a very small plaza between the main hall and its ancillary buildings. The northern staircase is striking since it is a covered staircase which rises from the former refectory at the ground level of this sub-temple of the Todai-ji to the elevated main hall of the Nigatsu-do. The raised main hall on its wooden pillars of support is surrounded by a walkway on all four sides, the main veranda on the west jutting out into the air higher than the other buildings of the Todai-ji below. The veranda provides a magnificent view over the massive roof of the Daibutsuden and the city of Nara and the valley with the mountains beyond it to the west.

The Nigatsu-do was built in 752 as a prayer for the recovery of the Emperor Shomu from an illness, the same illness which led to the earlier-than-anticipated dedication of the Daibutsu lest the emperor not live to see the completion of his grand project. The main images of the Nigatsu-do consist of a large and a small image of the Bodhisattva Kannon, both of them *hibutsu*. The smaller Kannon was found in the waters of Naniwa-wan (Osaka Bay) in the eighth century, and it is reputed always to be warm to the touch. Since the image is a hidden one, this cannot be ascertained and must be accepted on faith.

The Nigatsu-do, the Second Month Hall, is so-named from the ceremonies which occur here each February and March, the second month of the traditional lunar calendar. The Shuni-e Ceremony is one of the more colorful events in Nara, and it attracts thousands of people since it has always been regarded as marking the end of the winter season and the coming of spring. From the public viewpoint, the ceremony begins unostentatiously, for it involves the "withdrawal from the world" by eleven priests who go into seclusion from February 24 until March 13. Sequestered from society and away from contact with the polluting world for seventeen days, they are purified and spend their time carrying out ceremonies which have been followed for more than 1,200 years. From March 1 through March 12 they solemnly walk around the temple's hidden image of Kannon from noon to midnight reciting the Kannon's various names.

The ceremonies reach a climax in mid-March with the Torch Ceremony and then the special Water Drawing Ceremony. On March 11 and 12, the eleven priests return from their period of withdrawal from public life as they march about the outer galleries of the Nigatsu-do, each with a torch twenty-six feet long. Brandishing these huge flaming poles, they scatter the burning embers from the torches onto the crowds below, signifying the burning away of the viewers' transgressions and the bringing of good luck to those showered by the embers. Then at the conclusion of their period of seclusion on March 13, sacred water is drawn by the priests from the Wakasa well in the Akaiya well house below the temple, symbolizing the first waters of spring-time. Portions of this water are prized by the visitors to the ceremonies of these three days. With the conclusion of the Nigatsu-do ceremony, winter is traditionally at an end, and the public can look forward to the rebirth of life with the spring season.

KAISAN-DO

Abbot Roben was the chief priest of the Todai-ji during the period of its construction as well as a trusted confidant of the Emperor Shomu. It was he whom the emperor relied upon for spreading the Buddhist faith in Japan, and his influence is noted in many temples in the area around and even beyond Nara. When he died in 773, an image in the Sangatsu-do, the Shikkongo-shin, was dedicated to his memory, and as mentioned previously, it is only shown each year on the anniversary of Roben's death, December 16.

It is usual for a temple to dedicate a building to its founder, and this tradition has not gone unobserved at the Todai-ji. As a result, the Kaisan-do or Founder's Hall was created in 1250 just across from the Sangatsu-do. A minor building, compared to the others so far visited at the Todai-ji, its most important image is that of the abbot who is seated in traditional fashion. The abbot holds a *shaku*, a wand of authority traditionally held by officials of state and church. This particular *shaku* is of note since it is reputed to have belonged to the Emperor Shomu at one time. As an important reminder of the Todai-ji's illustrious history and the contribution of its first abbot not only to this particular temple but to the Buddhist faith in Japan, the doors to the case which holds the image of Abbot Roben are only opened each year on the anniversary of his birth on August 2.

SHORO AND OTHER BUILDINGS

Steps at the side of the Kaisan-do descend in two stages to the front of the Daibutsuden, and these steps take the visitor past some minor units of the Todai-ji. On the intermediate level, the steps lead to the Shoro, the open belfry which holds the temple bell. The bell is one of the oldest bells in Japan, and it is particularly noted as the bell which was used during the ceremonies in the 752 dedication of the Great Buddha image. The striking of the bell is a favorite act of visitors, and the deep tone for which the bell is noted can be heard throughout the temple grounds. The bell is 12.8 feet tall and has a circumference of twenty-seven feet. It is no lightweight, for its bronze body is 10.6 inches thick. It was damaged by the 1239 typhoon which swept through the temple grounds, destroying the wooden structure holding the bell and doing damage to the bell itself. It is thought that the bell may have been recast at this time due to the damage it sustained.

Clustered about the bell are three small buildings which are generally not open to the public. These consist of the Gyogi-do, the Nembutsu-do, and the Shunjo-do. The Nembutsu-do is the easternmost of the three buildings, and it is a small structure for the repetition of the *Nembutsu* prayer. In it is a seated Jizo image which was created in the 1190s by the sculptor Kosei. Adjacent is the Gyogi-do. Gyogi (668–749) was a priest of the Gango-ji temple who was assigned the task of raising a portion of the funds for the original Daibutsuden. As with many learned monks of his day, his knowledge of construction and engineering proved invaluable when technical help was needed in the building of the huge Great Buddha Hall. Gyogi has been remembered by a seated image of this early priest which is within the vermilion-and-white interior of this structure.

The third and last building about the Shoro is the Shunjo-do which was built to hold an image of the priest Chogen. If Gyogi was important in the initial construction of the Todai-ji, it is

Chogen who is remembered for his part in the reconstruction of the temple after the disastrous fires set by a Taira clan general which destroyed the temple in 1180. After the fire, it was Chogen who undertook the task of raising the funds needed to rebuild the Daibutsuden and to restore the Daibutsu, as well as for the replacement of numerous other Todai-ji buildings. His image, which has been traditionally kept in the Shunjo-do, is one of the most realistic and notable of the Todai-ji's many sculptures. The image shows the elderly monk in his last days, wizened and aged, fingering his rosary as he awaits his next rebirth or release into nirvana. An Amida Nyorai and an Aizen Myo-o image are at his side. The doors to the small building are opened on July 5 each year so visitors may see the realistic image of one of the saviors of the temple.

The steps continue their downward path, passing the golden Sorin-to en route to the front of the Daibutsuden. A *sorin* is the metal top to a pagoda (*to*), and this *sorin* serves as a reminder of the original pagoda which was topped by a *sorin* of the magnitude of the one which now stands on the hillside to the east of the Daibutsuden. This *sorin* was created for the Osaka International Fair of 1970 and was given to the temple after the fair ended.

The path down the hill ends at the eastern end of the Daibutsuden, and the path to Noborioji can be followed from the center of the corridor before the Daibutsuden and so through the great Nandai-mon gate to Noborioji, the main street of Nara.

TOUR

 3

Kofuku-ji
Kasuga Grand Shrine

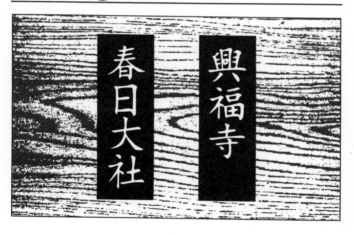

S ANJO-DORI (Third Avenue) was an important street in the second decade of the 700s when Fujiwara-no-Fuhito, the first minister of the imperial government, was carried along its way in his palanquin as he headed from the imperial palace to his family clan temple, the Kofuku-ji, and to the sacred Kasuga Shrine where the spirit of his clan progenitor had been brought on the back of a sacred deer. It is still an important if narrow street today, some 1,200 years later, since it now connects the Japan Rail Station with the same Kofuku-ji temple and Kasuga Shrine. It also happens to be a major shopping area of central Nara. (It can be reached from the Kintetsu Railway Nara Station by walking one street south through the covered, arcaded shopping street of Higashi-muki-dori at the station's southeast exit.)

The small shops along Sanjo-dori, Higashi-muki-dori, and its extension to the south as the covered Mochiidono-dori are fascinating since they encompass a number of different craft and antique shops as well as restaurants and other stores of a general nature. Konishi-dori, an even narrower shopping street parallel to and to the west of Higashi-muki-dori, has numerous shops and a small department store, and it is intriguing because of the variety of wares offered for sale along this narrow lane which offers the opportunity to rub shoulders with the local populace—its restricted width making for a congenial if crowded atmosphere. Another interesting street is the extension of Higashi-muki-dori to the north of Noborioji, a street whose shops deal more with local people than with tourists.

Sanjo-dori maintains a continuing connection with Nara's ancient past and its skilled artisans since it has antique shops and calligraphy materials suppliers where ink stones and writing brushes may be obtained. Among the craft stores on these three long streets between the Japan Rail Station and the Sarusawa Pond there has even, in recent years, been a shop which supplies materials for making American-style quilts! It also, in contrast to its few traditional shops, has the modern Fujita Hotel with its contemporary coffee shop. The Nara Tourist Information Center, which is a source of information to all visitors, is at the intersection midway along the route. All of these units provide that juxtaposition of the past and present which in Nara are never far apart. Behind the Fujita Hotel, for example, is a link with those centuries prior to the creation of Nara in 710, for here is the tomb of the early Emperor Kaika.

TOMB OF EMPEROR KAIKA

Just to the west of the Fujita Hotel, a path leads to the north and to the fenced-in, mounded tomb of the Emperor Kaika. According to legend, he was the ninth emperor, and it is claimed that he ascended the throne in his fiftieth year and then reigned for sixty years from 158 B.C. to 98 B.C. If tradition can be believed, he lived for 110 years, legendary emperors enjoying legendary longevity. Since mounded tombs, such as this emperor's tomb, were built between A.D. 300 and A.D. 700, either someone else is buried here or Kaika lived at a later date and possibly for a shorter life span than tradition has claimed.

When it comes to imperial tombs, one always has to regard them with the proverbial grain of salt. Official identification of imperial graves was only made in the late nineteenth century when Shinto militarists were intent upon enlarging upon the myths surrounding the imperial family—and any future, proper exploration of such tombs was forestalled then (and even now), since, in the days prior to 1945, investigators could be accused of *lèse majesté* in their desire to arrive at actual dates for such graves or to question the "facts" which the government had decreed as to who was buried in a specific spot. To believe the legends about early rulers can bring romantic pleasure—so long as one realizes that romance and truth too often reside primarily in the mind of the beholder.

Huge burial mounds such as this one are often called keyhole tombs since their shape resembles that of a modern keyhole. They were huge (the Emperor Nintoku's tomb in Osaka extends the length between two modern railroad stations), and they were surrounded by a water-filled moat. The coffin itself rested in a small stone chamber over which the earthen mound was raised, but such tombs were no longer created after the 700s when the Buddhist practice of cremation took hold. This tomb is, in a sense, a truncated one since it does not include a moat—but in its modern state it is indicative of the grandeur imposed on such imperial burial sites in the late nineteenth century when granite fences and torii were placed about such tombs to lend the appropriate dignity to former emperors. So standard were the forms of glory imparted to these grave sites that one could possibly credit the Meiji period of the late nineteenth century with having invented prefabricated construction.

NARA TOURIST INFORMATION CENTER

The Information Center is in a corner building at the end of the first stretch of Sanjo-dori when coming from the railway stations. It has multilingual agents, and it offers maps, brochures, and information concerning Nara and its surroundings, as well as lists of current activities in the area. It can also provide guide service, some of it without charge by knowledgeable English-speaking students who wish to practice their linguistic ability. The center has a fascinating large diorama showing what Nara looked like in the 700s, and the diorama offers a magnificent bird's-eye view of the grandeur which was Nara in its early days. Audio-visual presentations provide information on sites of interest while a display of crafts and other items created in Nara today line the walls and fill the exhibit cases.

SARUSAWA POND

At the east end of the shopping portion of Sanjo-dori, the Sarusawa Pond with its 393-yard circumference comes into view. On the left (to the north) of Sanjo-dori is the rise on which the Kofuku-ji temple sits, while to the right of the street is the Sarusawa Pond and some of the many *ryokan* of the area.

The Sarusawa Pond is a pleasant place to rest on one of the benches along its circular pathway (or to have a picnic lunch), for it offers the traditional scene so often depicted in woodblock prints of Nara: the pond, the willow trees, and across the pond and reflected in its waters the lofty pagoda of the Kofuku-ji temple rising in the background. For the Japanese it has an additional fascination aside from its beauty, for the pond is connected with a love suicide, the kind of romantic story which has endeared itself to sentimental Japanese across the years.

The Lady Uneme, who is the heroine and victim of this tale, is said to have served in the 700s as a lady-in-waiting to an emperor (a most pleasant euphemism for the emperor's romantic needs). This court beauty was desired by many of the courtiers of the day, all of whom she spurned out of her at first unrequited love for the emperor. Her affection was in time—and all too briefly—rewarded by the emperor until his jaded interests led him from her. Having lost the affection of the emperor, the love-lorn lady hung her clothes on a willow tree at the side of the Sarusawa Pond

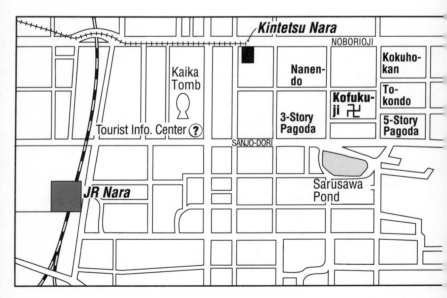

and drowned herself in its still waters. Lady Uneme might long since have been forgotten, but her desperate act has been remembered in a commemorative celebration which takes place each mid-September on the night of the full moon. A procession in eighth-century costumes has as its destination the Sarusawa Pond, and there traditional music is offered, and, afterwards, flowers are strewn on the waters of the pond from a colorful dragon-headed boat in memory of the Lady Uneme. Under the trees at one corner of the pond, a commemorative stone (the Uneme Shrine) tells the sad story (in Japanese) of the Lady Uneme, while one willow tree at the east side of the pond is known as the Coat Hanging Willow since this is ostensibly where the lady hung her clothes before plunging to her death.

KOFUKU-JI

A broad staircase leads up from the Sarusawa Pond to the grounds of the Kofuku-ji temple, the earliest temple in the new

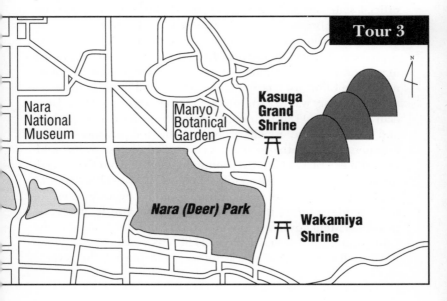

capital and seat of the Hosso sect of Buddhism. The Kofuku-ji (Happiness Producing Temple) was a complex of Buddhist structures of which Fujiwara-no-Fuhito, the first minister of the court, could be justifiably proud. Not only had he brought the imperial court and the capital to the newly created city of Heijo-kyo (Nara) in 710, but that same year he moved his family temple (now renamed the Kofuku-ji) to Nara from its former site in the previous capital of Fujiwara-kyo, some twenty miles to the south. In its new location, the Fujiwara clan temple stood on a prominence to the east of the city in a section which became known as the Outer Capital where it overlooked Nara and the imperial palace to the west below it.

The temple in its early years never lacked for magnificence. Since he was the leading minister of government to whom the imperial rulers were indebted, Fuhito's temple was endowed with splendid buildings by members of the imperial family and the state. At the height of its glory, 175 buildings enriched the leading clan temple in Nara. The Kofuku-ji was ranked with the official state temples, and government support was generous. The temple boasted not only the usual halls of worship and monastic outbuildings, but it served as well as a hospital, an orphanage, a home for old people, and it had a public bathhouse in addition to maintaining a university on its grounds. It epitomized the Buddhist charitable concern for all living beings.

All this glory was to turn to ashes in time. Destroyed by a Taira clan general in 1180 (the same general who destroyed Todai-ji and laid waste to much of Nara), the temple was rebuilt. Frequent fires in other centuries continued to destroy its buildings, the fire of 1717 almost wiping the temple from the map in more recent times. Fortunately, much of its post-1180 art work has been saved despite the continuing series of catastrophes. In more modern times, the temple suffered grievously under the post-1870 Meiji government with its anti-Buddhist leanings. The Chu-kondo, the Central Golden Hall, was confiscated so as to serve as the Nara Prefectural Offices; the Jiki-do, the temple refectory, was turned into a public school; and in 1881 the temple's lands were seized to create a public park. All of the famed sculptures of the temple were then crowded into the small Nanen-do and the Hokuen-do, and many of the temple treasures and sutras were destroyed. Its companion Kasuga Shrine was separated completely from the temple despite its 1,100 years of close association.

Fortunately, the granting of religious freedom after 1945 has permitted the slow restoration of the temple, a task which someday may see a further re-creation of its lost or damaged buildings. Then in 1958 a postwar government, realizing the richness of the treasures of the temple and their place in the religious and artistic heritage of the middle ages, built the fireproof treasure hall, the Kokuho-kan, to safeguard and display the temple sculptures.

FIVE-STORY PAGODA

At the top of the fifty-two steps from the Sarusawa Pond is the five-story pagoda of the Kofuku-ji. Originally built in 730 at the request of the Empress Komyo, it has burned to the ground on five occasions, and the present 166-foot-tall pagoda was erected in 1426. It is second in height only to the To-ji temple pagoda in Kyoto. Four Buddha images are enshrined at its base: Sakyamuni, the historic Buddha, on the south side; Amida, the Buddha of the Western Paradise on the west side; Yakushi Buddha, the Healing Buddha and Buddha of the Joruri or Eastern Paradise on the east; and Miroku, the Buddha of the Future on the north side. One of the favorite Japanese pastimes from the early Nara years of the 700s to the present day has been the viewing of the pagoda and its reflection in the Sarusawa Pond by autumn moonlight.

TO-KONDO

To the north of the five-story pagoda is the To-kondo (East Golden Hall) erected in 726 at the wish of the Emperor Shomu. It has been destroyed by fire five times, and its present building is a 1415 reconstruction along its original lines. The To-kondo is usually a secondary worship hall in most temples of this early period, but with the destruction and sometimes confiscation of the Kofuku-ji's main halls, the To-kondo has become the primary hall of worship for the temple.

The main image of the To-kondo is an 8.4-foot Yakushi Nyorai, the Buddha of Medicine and of Healing, from 1400. He is accompanied by 9.8-foot bronze Nikko and Gakko Bodhisattvas of the late 600s, images stolen by the Kofuku-ji's warrior-monks in 1185 from the Yamada-dera temple in Asuka, some twenty miles to the south. Upset over the loss of their own temple's images in the 1180 fire, the monks resorted to strong-arm tactics to replace the images which had been destroyed when the To-kondo burned. Thus the Yamada-dera Yakushi and his companion Nikko and Gakko figures became the center of the rebuilt Kofuku-ji To-kondo. The Nikko and Gakko remain, the Yamada-dera Yakushi having been destroyed in a later fire, except for its head which is now in the temple treasure hall. Six out of the temple's Twelve Heavenly Generals from 1207 stand guard behind Yakushi, the other six being on view in the treasure house. To the left of Yakushi is an image of Monju from the 1100s, a youthful-looking deity with an unusual topknot of hair which supports a sacred casket. To the right of the Yakushi is a Yuima-koji, a contemporary disciple of the historic Buddha, carved by the noted sculptor Jokei in 1194. A ninth-century Komoku-ten Guardian King is at the left rear of the image platform while a companion Jikoku-ten is at the left foreground. These latter two images are two of the Four Guardian Kings who protect the Buddhist faith.

CHU-KONDO

The Chu-kondo (Middle Golden Hall) has burned down on numerous occasions since its 710 construction. The present building is a "temporary" hall from 1819, and it is in such poor repair that it is closed to the public. (It is the building which served as the Nara Prefectural Office after the 1870s confiscation.) Its main image of Sakyamuni as well as a Yakushi image and four Shitenno have thus been placed in the building behind the Chu-kondo, a comparatively recent building which is only open to the public for a brief period in the spring and fall.

NANEN-DO

To the west of the Chu-kondo at some distance is a 1789 reconstruction of a ninth-century hall, the Nanen-do (South Octagonal Hall). It is the twelfth of the Kannon pilgrimage temples in western Japan, and thus it is much visited by the devout even though their prayers today have to be said from outside this seldom opened building. Its main image is a Fukukensaku Kannon which was surrounded by the Six Patriarchs of the Hosso sect of Buddhism (now in the treasure hall), and it was originally protected by four Shitenno (now also in the treasure hall). The Nanen-do is open to the public on October 17 annually at which time the Kannon with his "never empty lasso" with which he saves individuals is on view. On the south side of the building is a small image of Jizo, the deity who protects children, and worshippers can often be seen dousing the statue with water as an act of worship. Behind the Nanen-do is the temple's three-story pagoda from 1143 which still retains its interior paintings of the traditional one thousand Buddha images.

HOKUEN-DO

The Hokuen-do (North Octagonal Hall) is a 1210 reconstruction of the original 721 structure, and this impressive octagonal hall was created a year after the death of Fujiwara-no-Fuhito (659–720), the founder of Nara and civil ruler under various monarchs, as a memorial to his spirit. Its main image, in a setting of orange brocaded drapes, is the Miroku Nyorai, the Buddha of the Future, which was created in the early 1200s. Four images of the founders of the Hosso sect of Buddhism (one of the earliest of the Buddhist sects to be brought to Japan) stand beside and behind Miroku. The two images at the rear are of Mujaku and Seshin and are by the sculptor Unkei; they are considered to be his masterpieces and among the finest pieces of wood sculpture of the 1200s. The hall is open at special times in the spring and fall as can be ascertained at the Tourist Information Center since these times change annually.

KOKUHO-KAN

The Kokuho-kan is the fairly recent (1958) Kofuku-ji treasure hall, and it is one of Japan's great treasuries of early Buddhist sculpture. It contains many of the temple's major works created by the most noted artists in the period after the 1180 destruction of the temple by fire: Jocho, Kokei, Unkei, Kaikei, Jokei, and Koben. The masterpieces are so numerous in the hall that only a few of the more notable ones can be mentioned here.

Head of Yakushi Nyorai This cast-bronze head from A.D. 680 is all that remains of the main image of the Yamada-dera temple, an image which the Kofuku-ji warrior-monks stole from the Yamada-dera in 1185. This stolen Yakushi image was destroyed in a later Kofuku-ji fire, and the head was only discovered as late as 1937 resting under the image platform of the To-kondo where it had been since the 1415 rebuilding of this temple building. The magnificent three-foot-tall head with its full features is one of the finest examples of Tang Chinese influenced sculpture in Japan.

Hachibu-shu The Eight Classes of Divine Protectors were created about the year 734. Most noted among them is the multi-arm, dry-lacquer image of Ashura. This most graceful statue with a winsome face on three sides of its head is, along with the bronze head of the Yakushi Nyorai, worth a visit to this hall if for no other reason.

Kongo Rikishi These two muscular, scowling protectors of the temple are among the most famous such images in Japan, and they are among the noted masterpieces of wood sculpture of the Kamakura period (1185–1333). More than life-size, their fury matches their stature. Once the guardians before the temple's portals, today they stand on either side of the entrance and exit doors to the treasure hall.

Tentoki and Ryutoki If the Yakushi Nyorai head is most impressive, the Ashura most winsome, and the Kongo Rikishi the fiercest of images, then these two stocky, muscular demons of 1215 by Koben are, in their humorous appearance, the most delightful images in the treasury. Tentoki is a ferocious-looking demon who is holding a large lantern aloft with one hand as though showing off his strength. Ryutoki balances a lantern on his head, his eyes cast upward as if he were wondering if the object will stay there. One wonders also, under the strain of his maintaining the lantern in place, whether his skimpy loincloth will long remain about his body. As demons go, these two are captivating!

HONBO AND OYUYA

A path between the To-kondo and the five-story pagoda leads to the east toward the Kasuga Shrine. Along the way are the temple offices, the Honbo, on the left, and the Oyuya, the temple bathhouse for the monks, on the right. The Oyuya was rebuilt in 1415, and in its earthen floor are two large cauldrons, possibly cast in 1117, for the heating of the bath water—a bathing amenity which originally was available to the townspeople as well as the monks. There are louvered, open windows in the upper walls to let the smoke of the heating fires flow out. The bath is now a historic unit, modern monks having more recent and less smoky facilities.

DEER PARK

The path to the east from the Oyuya leads into the park-like grounds of the Kasuga Grand Shine and the Nara Deer Park. The Kasuga Grand Shrine has been associated with deer since its reputed founding by Fujiwara-no-Fuhito in 709. As a result, some one thousand deer can still be encountered throughout the shrine grounds and about the nearby Todai-ji temple. The deer were always permitted to wander freely in Nara since they were considered the sacred messengers of the gods, and at one time the killing of a deer was penalized by the execution of the miscreant responsible for the death of an animal. In the era of automobiles which pose a continuing danger to does and bucks who meander indiscriminately onto local highways, this penalty is fortunately no longer observed.

If there is one souvenir which is ubiquitous in Nara and is a reminder of the Deer Park, it is that of the commercial representations of deer which are available at shops and outdoor stalls in Nara. One finds them carved in wood (which are sometimes quite attractive), and one finds them as repugnant red plastic, blown-up does and bucks which, naturally, are a delight to children.

To the right of the main path into the Kasuga Shrine grounds, halfway along the route to the shrine buildings, is a small path which leads to the enclosed field and amphitheater where bucks are de-horned each October so as to obviate danger to each other (and to visitors to the park) during their combative rutting season. On the de-horning occasion, the deer attendants lasso and tie the bucks in a rodeo-like event in front of the spectators in the amphitheater as a preliminary to the removing of their horns. Adjacent to the ampitheater are the pens where the deer are gathered each night throughout the year for feeding and watering.

The deer have long been sacred in Nara since it is claimed that the four Shinto kami of the Kasuga Shrine were first brought to Nara on the back of sacred deer. According to legend, the main divinity of the shrine, Ame-no-Koyane, the Fujiwara tutelary spirit, arrived in Nara on the back of a white deer in 709, and he was later joined in 768 by the three other kami who were transported in like manner. The four have always been known collectively as the Kasuga Myojin or Kasuga Gongen, and each deity has its own small shrine building in the Kasuga's inner shrine area.

In 1135, Ame-no-Koyane and his spouse (one of the other three kami at the shrine) had a son, the Wakamiya (Young Prince), and a separate shrine (the Kasuga Wakamiya Shrine) was built for him to the southeast of the Kasuga Shrine. The deities of the Kasuga Shrine also served as the Shinto protectors of the Kofuku-ji temple, and in time the shrine was virtually absorbed by the more hierarchically structured administration of the Buddhist temple it protected. In 1868, however, the Meiji government forced the separation of all shrines and temples, and it favored the Shinto shrines, often to the detriment of Buddhist temples.

The main route into the Kasuga Shrine grounds follows the path which begins at the eastern end of Sanjo-dori as well as the path from the Kofuku-ji, mentioned earlier in this tour, which joins this main route. At the entrance to the 213-acre forested area is the first torii, erected in 836, and this leads after eight-tenths of a mile across fields and through groves of cryptomeria trees to the second torii of 1160 opposite the treasure hall. The most striking thing about the path as one progresses further into the shrine grounds is the profusion of stone lanterns which line the way. Some two thousand free-standing lanterns grace the shrine grounds, all gifts of the devout, while another one thousand metal lanterns can be found hanging from the eaves of temple buildings, also gifts to the shrine.

Early in the year on the night of February 3–4 at the Setsubun Festival, when winter officially comes to an end, the lanterns of the shrine are lit. On this evening the shrine *miko,* young women attendants at the shrine, perform the stately Bugaku dances by torchlight in their wide, split red skirt over a white undergarment. Again on the evening of August 15 at the Manto-e

Ceremony the lanterns are lit once more just as they were during the February lantern celebration.

MANYO BOTANICAL GARDEN

Halfway along the path into the Kasuga Shrine, as the main path begins to bend to the right, is the Manyo Botanical Garden on the left. The garden harks back to those early years of Nara since an attempt has been made to bring together all of the plants which were mentioned in the *Manyoshu,* a collection of poems which were gathered in 759. Three hundred plants which brightened the lives of both courtiers and commoners in the eighth century can here be enjoyed, and they are labeled with both their Latin and their Japanese names. A rivulet wanders through the garden, and it is crossed by an arched vermillion bridge to give the ambiance of an eighth-century pleasance or noble garden. This ambiance is further enhanced by a platform in the middle of the garden pond, a stage which is used for presentation of the traditional Bugaku dances on May 5 and November 3. When one has become sated with flowers of the eighth century, to the left of the garden is the Ninai-jaya, a tea room with outdoor tables where refreshments may be enjoyed.

At the end of the main portion of the path to the Kasuga Shrine, a series of lanterns line the broad steps leading to the slope to the Chakuto-den, the reception hall for the imperial messenger, on the left. Beginning in 916, this structure served as the place where the emperor's delegate to the March 13 Kasuga Matsuri would be received, and here today on March 13, at the shrine's annual festival, the reception of the imperial messenger is re-enacted as a part of the day's festivities. On this occasion the shrine priests in ancient costume perform the stately Yamato-mai dance, and Bugaku is performed as well.

At the top of the steps the path diverges, the right-hand portion leading to the Kasuga Wakamiya Shrine while the left-hand section leads to the Nandai-mon, the Great South Gate, of the Kasuga inner shrine.

KASUGA GRAND SHRINE

INNER SHRINE

The two-story vermillion-and-white Nandai-mon provides an impressive entry into the Kasuga inner shrine, a spacious area enclosed within a roofed corridor with eight gates. Ahead, before the rising ground leading to the innermost shrine buildings is a cypress-bark-roofed structure without walls and with a dirt floor. This is the Haiden (offertory) which traditionally stands before the inner shrine and where offerings and religious services to the gods are held. It was here that the daimyo, the territorial lords of the Tokugawa period (1603–1868), came to worship, and here the traditional scattering of beans to scare away evil takes place on February 3. To the left of the Haiden is the Buden, a "gold" covered ceremonial floor where religious dances are offered to the kami. Adjoining it on the left is the wall-less, wood-floored Naorai-den, the Hall of Enlightenment, which is also used for religious services. Behind it is the westernmost of the four corridors about the inner shrine.

On either side of the Nandai-mon are counters where Shinto religious materials may be purchased. The counter on the right is also where one may pay for entry to the corridor to the right of the Nandai-mon entry, a corridor which leads to the Chu-mon or Central Gate atop the slope above the Haiden. The Chu-mon both screens and is the entry to the innermost shrine area where the four individual shrines of the Kasuga Myojin are located. The first shrine to the east is that of Takemikazuchi; the next is of Futsu-nushi; the third is that of Ame-no-Koyane, the progenitor of the Fujiwara clan; and the fourth one is that of his wife, Hime-gami. These separate small shrine buildings have *chigi*, crossed beams, extending from the front to the rear of the peak of the shrine roof. *Chigi* with a flat top indicate that the kami within is a female. *Chigi* without a flat top indicate that a male deity is enshrined.

To the left of the shrines, beyond the Naorai-den, is the

Utsushidono, the Transfer Hall, where the deities are housed during the periodic rebuilding of these shrines. Traditionally the shrines should be rebuilt every twenty years, a tradition no longer here maintained, the last rebuilding occurring in 1957 after a lapse of many generations. The passageway between the western corridor and the Utsushidono is lined with hanging metal lanterns whose dark-bronze finish contrasts sharply with the bright vermilion of the shrine wood, the white of the plaster walls, and the green of the bars over the windows of the corridor and the buildings.

KASUGA TREASURE HOUSES

The Kasuga Shrine has two treasure houses, the older one being to the west of the western corridor of the inner shrine area. The new, ferro-concrete treasury is opposite the second torii along the main entry path, and it houses some four thousand items from the year 646, the year the Fujiwara clan received its present name of Fujiwara (Wisteria Grove)—from the grove atop Tonomine hill in the Asuka region where Fujiwara-no-Fuhito's father together with the prince who became the Emperor Tenchi plotted the overthrow of the dictatorial Soga civil rulers—to 794 when Kyoto became the capital of Japan. Here on view are Bugaku masks, shrine regalia, scrolls, musical instruments, armor, swords, and mirrors among other items of the shrine heritage. One section of the old treasury building is particularly interesting, for it houses the huge ceremonial drums used in shrine festivities, and one wall of the building has to be slid from place to permit the removal of these gigantic units.

KASUGA WAKAMIYA SHRINE

At the top of the steps leading to the Nandai-mon, the path to the right heads to the Shrine of the Young Prince (Wakamiya), the son of Ame-no-Koyane and Hime-gami of the Kasuga Shrine. The 1135 Kasuga Wakamiya is a very simple shrine, as are most Shinto shrines. Its main hall is a low, one-story building of thirteen bays which is divided into three parts and which stands before the roofed, wall-less Haiden (offertory). The southern section of this thirteen-bay structure is the Kagura-den where the shrine *miko* perform the Bugaku dances at the December 17–18 shrine festival, a festival which dates back to 1136, the year after the shrine was created. The middle section is the Miro, a connecting unit between the two end sections, while the third portion is the Hosodono, the platform on which the musicians sit. This latter portion is divided into two sections, half of which is tatami-matted for the musicians. The small one-bay Honden, the shrine housing the spirit of the Young Prince, lies behind a fence opposite the Haiden. It was last rebuilt in 1863.

To the north of the main hall of the shrine is the Chujuya with a cypress-bark roof. Its interior walls are covered with rice paddles which visitors have used as *ema* plaques on which to write their prayers. Rice paddles have been used as *ema* at other shrines as well since one of the major concerns of the Shinto deities has been for the well-being of the rice crop, rice having been the mainstay of the Japanese diet for centuries. The Kasuga Shrine still honors the importance of rice, and on March 15 each year there is a Rice Planting Ceremony when the shrine rice field is symbolically planted. A stove in the Chujuya indicates that the building was probably used as a refectory at one time.

The Wakamiya Festival of December 16–17 is one of the highlights of Nara's festival season. Traditional Japanese religious dances, plays, and farces are presented, and these include Bugaku, Noh, Kyogen, and Dengaku. Shrine *miko* in their long red skirts and white blouses perform the stately Kagura dance to the accompaniment of flutes, *hyoshigi* (wooden clappers), koto, *sho* (Pan pipes), and hand drums while the shrine priests separately perform the Yamato-mai dance. On December 17 there is a long procession of warriors and courtiers of the past who march from the Kofuku-ji temple to the shrine in eighth-century costumes.

The Kofuku-ji temple and the Kasuga Shrine remained the

ancestral places of worship for the Fujiwara family whose contribution to Japanese life continued down through the years. Fujiwara daughters for centuries were intermarried into the imperial family, a practice which was only discontinued in modern times.

TOUR

 4

Yakushi-ji
Toshodai-ji
Daian-ji

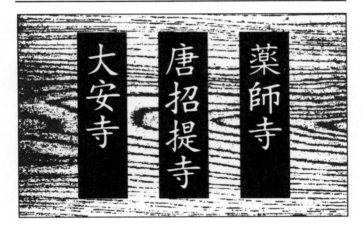

WHILE the Kofuku-ji, the clan temple of the Fujiwara, was the first temple to be built in Nara in 710, due to the political influence of Fujiwara-no-Fuhito, the three other major temples of the former capital at Fujiwara-kyo were quick to move to the new capital of Heijo-kyo (Nara) as well, so as not to lose political or religious influence at the court. Buddhism was still so new to Japan, having gained its foothold barely a century earlier, and since it was still of influence only at the court, that remaining in the abandoned former capital would have meant a slow death to any temple which remained behind, as was the case with the Kawara-dera which did not move and which today is merely an archeological site. Thus it was that the Yakushi-ji temple moved to the southwest edge of Heijo-kyo while the Asuka-dera moved to the southeast corner of the new capital under its new name of the Gango-ji, and the Daikandai-ji temple became the Daian-ji in the south-central portion of Heijo-kyo.

Time, in the long run, did not deal kindly with the Daian-ji or the Gango-ji, and these once powerful and rich temples are today a very pale reflection of their one-time glorious past. They each have come down to but one or two buildings and a fireproof treasure hall, their pagodas, their Kondo or golden halls but a memory. The lone survivor of the Four Great Temples of the Asuka region of the seventh century is the Yakushi-ji which in the second half of the twentieth century has come into flower once more under dynamic religious leadership.

In this tour we shall cover the Yakushi-ji, the Toshodai-ji, which did not come into being until after Nara Buddhism began a new flourishing under Emperor Shomu in the mid-eighth century, and the Daian-ji which today is a mere shadow.

YAKUSHI-JI

The Yakushi-ji temple had its beginnings in the former capital of Fujiwara-kyo under the Emperor Temmu (reigned 673–686). The emperor, who enjoyed certain noble privileges, had a number of consorts, but when his chief wife, the future Empress Jito, developed a serious eye disease in 680, the concerned emperor ordered the building of a temple in the Asuka region to the Buddha Yakushi, the Buddha of Healing and Medicine, as a plea for the improved health of his chief consort. Perhaps the emperor's intent was enough to satisfy the Buddha, for the future Empress Jito's condition did improve even before the construction of the temple began. Once construction was underway, however, it was another seventeen years before the temple was completed, and its completion was only consummated eleven years after the death of the emperor. The emperor's consort Jito, ruling as his successor, ultimately had the temple completed for the sake of the emperor's soul in his next existence.

Only two decades later in 710 the court moved from Fujiwara-kyo in the Asuka region to Nara twenty miles to the north, and thus the Yakushi-ji began a new life in 718 in the southwest corner of the new capital. It was 726 before the major construction of this splendid temple was completed, although its pagoda did not receive its final finial until 730. Occupying a twelve-block-square portion of the new city, it was the only temple which retained its Fujiwara-kyo configuration—a configuration which, interestingly enough, is being completely re-established in the second half of the twentieth century.

Fire, of course, is the enemy of all wooden structures in a land given to earthquakes and civil conflict. In time, only the eastern of the temple's two pagodas remained, a fire in the sixteenth century wiping out all the early buildings with the exception of the To-to, the East Pagoda. This was an unfortunate time for the temple's destruction, since the Tokugawa shogunate (1603–1868) slighted this historic temple, while the Meiji government (1868–1912) was antagonistic to all Buddhist temples. Thus the Yakushi-ji began a long decline in the late 1500s, a decline from which it has only been rescued since the 1970s when a new abbot, Koin Takeda, began the revitalization and rebuilding of the temple complex.

The Yakushi-ji can be reached most easily by taking the local train (not the express) from platform five of Yamato Saidai-ji Station (the second station to the west of Kintetsu Nara Station). The second station after Yamato Saidai-ji is the Nishi-no-kyo ("West of the Capital") Station from which it is but a half block to the east to the entrance of the Yakushi-ji. Bus 63 from the bus station on Noborioji takes one in about fifteen minutes right to the Yakushi-ji temple while bus 52 leaves one on the highway at the Yakushi-mae bus stop (as announced in English over the bus loudspeaker) from which one walks west toward the rail line and the temple entrance.

The minor problem with these approaches is that the entrance at which one arrives happens to be the north or rear entrance to the temple. To approach the temple properly, one should enter from its south gate—and thus we will assume that you have walked quickly through the temple grounds so as to approach the temple buildings from the south as its founders anticipated. This also provides an opportunity to look quickly and briefly at the two Shinto shrines just across the road from the temple to the south, shrines which offer the protection of the Shinto gods to the temple.

INARI AND HACHIMAN SHRINES

The two Shinto shrines across from the temple conform to the normal Shinto shrine layout, and thus it cannot be said that they are particularly noteworthy—except for the fact that they own two of the oldest images of Shinto kami. Since Shinto never had created images of its deities, these carved figures are most unusual and were created about the year 800, obviously under the influence of Buddhist sculptural models.

One of the images represents Hachiman, the Shinto God of War, created in the unlikely form of a seated Buddhist priest. Hachiman is the deified spirit of the Emperor Ojin, an emperor who is one of those anomalies of early folk religion. According to tradition, he was the fifteenth emperor of Japan, and he is recorded as having lived from 201 to 312 (and reigned uneventfully for sixty of his one hundred and eleven years), thereby matching his great-grandfather, the Emperor Kaika's, legendary 110 years. Perhaps his longevity had something to do with the long period of gestation in his mother's womb.

Having determined to invade Korea despite her advanced state of pregnancy, his mother, the Empress Jingu, tied a stone to her abdomen with a sash so as to delay her child's birth. Her journey to Korea by boat was fortunate in that the god Sumiyoshi served as the ship's pilot, if the ancient records are correct, and, when a terrible storm occurred, large fishes rose from the depths of the sea to support the ship in the great waves which lay siege to the boat. Having won her war against Korea, she refrained from giving birth until she was back in Japan. With such a remarkable beginning in life (despite the fact that Ojin is reputed to have been a peaceful man), it is perhaps not surprising that he is honored in the Shinto pantheon as Hachiman, the God of War, and the patron of the Minamoto clan who later ruled as shoguns from Kamakura.

The other Shinto image belonging to the shrine is that of Kashi-dai Myojin, the name of the Empress Jingu once she entered the Shinto pantheon. These two images, and a third one of Nakatsu-hime (Ojin's consort), may occasionally be seen in the annual opening of the Yakushi-ji treasure hall when they are placed on display there.

NANDAI-MON

The original Nandai-mon or southern gate to the Yakushi-ji disappeared in a sixteenth-century fire, and the gate which replaced it has been a temporary one. It will eventually be replaced with a reconstructed version of the original Nandai-mon under Abbot Takeda's long-range plans. Once one passes through this gate into the temple grounds, the rebuilt Chu-mon or central gate of 1984 is traversed, a gate from which the Kairo or surrounding corridors will again envelop the main buildings of the temple as they originally did. Beyond the Chu-mon, to the east and west, stand the two pagodas, the Sai-to and the To-to, the West and the East Pagodas, while further ahead lies the Kondo, the golden or main hall, with the Toin-do, the Chinese hall, to the east.

PAGODAS

The Yakushi-ji was the first temple to have two pagodas, thereby marking a change in temple orientation. The earlier Buddhist temples in Japan had a single pagoda which lay beyond the Chu-

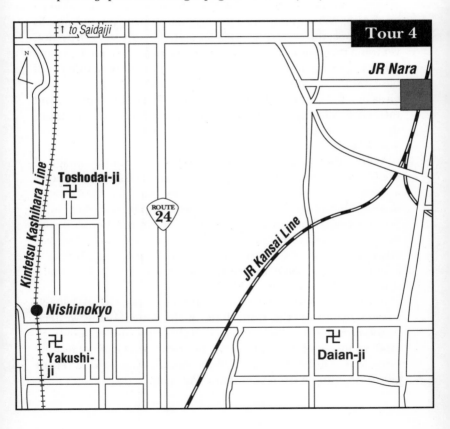

mon, and it marked the center of the religious complex inasmuch as relics (a portion of the ashes) of the Buddha Gautama were buried in its foundation under the main pillar which supported the pagoda. With the passage of time, a greater emphasis was placed on the Kondo, with its bronze Buddhist images. (No doubt with the creation of additional temples throughout Japan, there were insufficient relics to occupy the base of additional pagodas.) Thus the Yakushi-ji with its two pagodas to the side of the main courtyard reflects this change in emphasis.

After the conflagrations of past centuries, only the eastern pagoda of 730 remains of all the original Yakushi-ji buildings. In appearance, the eastern pagoda seems to be a six-story structure, yet it is a three-story pagoda whose extra *mokoshi* (roofs) give it a more imposing look. The pagoda is 112 feet tall on a thirty-foot base, and it was topped by a 32.8-foot metal *sorin* (spire) which ends in a 6.2-foot lacy finial with images of celestial dancers and musicians playing upon flutes and harps, one of the more delightful finials to any pagoda *sorin* in Japan (the original *sorin* is now in the Toin-do).

Within the open doors of the pagoda base is a small image of the Buddha flanked by two bodhisattvas, and before these images are some 150 small wooden stupas. In the year 764, the Empress Koken/Shotoku had one million of these stupas created to pacify the souls of soldiers who had been killed on her behalf in the putting down of a civil uprising. Each of the ten major temples was granted 100,000 of these tiny stupas, each stupa having a printed prayer inside it. These prayers are the oldest extant printed material in the world.

To the west of the To-to is the 1980 Sai-to (West Pagoda) which was re-created on the stone base of the long-missing western pagoda, and it stands out in its brilliant vermilion color. A modern image of the Buddha can be seen within each of its four sides, and at its base are relics of the Buddha Gautama, a recent gift to the temple from Gandhara, Pakistan.

KONDO

Central to the Yakushi-ji complex is the brilliant vermilion Kondo, the golden or main hall, with its noted bronze images. Earlier Kondo of the temple have been destroyed by fire, and after the 1528 fire a "temporary" Kondo of little note was erected in the 1600s, one which lasted until the 1970s since the temple could not afford to build a replacement. In 1975, Abbot Takeda saw to the re-creation of today's magnificent vermilion Kondo which houses the early main images of the temple. Funds were raised for the restoration of the hall through financial donations by the devout who made copies of the *Heart Sutra,* copies now in the new Sanzo-in.

The facade of the Kondo offers a dramatic picture: the vermilion-colored wood of its structure is set off by its white plaster walls, pierced on the main level by three huge sets of doors. When these doors are open, they reveal the bronze Buddha Yakushi and the Nikko and Gakko Bodhisattvas to either side of him, black against their golden aureoles, all set off by the vermilion framing of the exterior structure.

The Yakushi triad were once covered with a gold patina, but today they bear a magnificent glossy, ebony tone, the result of the 1528 fire. As examples of sculpture, they are a crowning achievement of the late 600s. Reflecting the full-bodied early Tang sculptural style of China, the images consist of the 8.4-foot seated Yakushi Nyorai, Lord of the Joruri (Eastern) Paradise and the Buddha of Medicine and Healing. His associates are the 10.5-foot Nikko and Gakko Bodhisattvas, the Bodhisattvas of the Sun and of the Moon. Cast in a relaxed stance with flowing drapery cascading from their bare upper torsos, and with detailed necklaces about their necks and chests, each bodhisattva has a hole in its forearm from which scarves once descended.

The Yakushi image is seated upon a medicine chest instead of the traditional lotus blossom, and therefore he does not bear the conventional medicine pot in his left hand. The 4.9-foot medicine chest is unique since its decorations represent designs which spread from the various cultural and artistic traditions between the Mediterranean and the Pacific. The grapevine scroll pattern at the edge of the upper frame is similar to Greek designs; the lotus flower usage can be seen in Moslem mosques of the Middle East; the twelve primitive figures of people in the arches of the base are found in Hindu temples in India (some see these as representing the Twelve Vows of Yakushi to save all sentient beings); while the dragon, the phoenix, the tiger, and the tortoise figured designs are familiar forms of Chinese Tang decoration. The chest thus shows the influence of the great Silk Road. Above the seated Yakushi is a canopy enlivened with stylized flowers in green and blue against a white background framed by vermilion-painted wood, a fringe of red and green beads hanging from the canopy.

BUSSOKU-SEKI

Within the Kondo on its west side (although these may be placed in a separate structure) is a stone dating from 752. It is incised with an outline of the Buddha's foot on which are inscribed *horin* (circles of truth). Such designs of the Buddha's footprint predate the use of Buddha images, the creation of Buddha images being a Greek influence upon Indian Buddhism. A 6.2-foot memorial stele from 752 is next to the footprint, and it has twenty-one verses in Japanese (written with Chinese characters) praising the footprint. It is thought that in times past these verses may have been chanted by devotees while circling the footprint stone.

TOIN-DO

To the east of the To-to, the East Pagoda, is the Toin-do, a 1285 rebuilding of what originally was a 721 hall. Its major image is an attractive 6.2-foot Sho Kannon in the form of a graceful young man standing before a large aureole whose gold leaf acts as a foil to the dark image. The Sho Kannon is a representation of the original Kannon before this bodhisattva manifested himself in his thirty-three different modes. The finial of the East Pagoda

△ The new pagoda at Yakushi-ji.

△ Yakushi-ji Kondo.
▽ Stone Buddhas at Hannya-ji.

△ Kofuku-ji pagoda reflected in Sarusawa Pond.

△ Todai-ji
Hachiman Shrine.

▷ Incense burner in front
of Todai-ji Daibutsuden.

▼ Row of lanterns at
Kasuga Grand Shrine.

◀ Kasuga Grand Shrine.

△ Hannya-ji.

▷ Binzuru statue outside
Todai-ji Daibutsuden.

▶ Nio statue at entrance
to Horyu-ji.

◀ Horyu-ji.

△ Hannya-ji pagoda.

with its musicians against the "splashing water" or simulated flames of the finial is now on display in the Toin-do as is a copy of the original picture of Kichijo-ten which is held in the temple treasure hall.

KODO
Behind the Kondo is the 1852 Kodo or lecture hall which is soon to be replaced by a more imposing structure. It holds a Yakushi triad also, this one from the 1200–1300s but of inferior workmanship to the images in the Kondo. Benches on either side of the altar are for the use of the monks when the abbot lectures on religious matters. It is in this hall that the service of The Turning of the Sutras is celebrated on the eighth day of each month. Behind the Kodo are the Kuri, the priests' quarters, and an orientation center and rest hall for the reception of groups of worshippers. In the northeast corner of the temple grounds, behind the reception hall, is the temple treasure house.

DAIHOZODEN
The Daihozoden, the treasure house of the Yakushi-ji, is open from October 20 to November 10 and from January 1 to 10 each year for the public showing of a selection of the temple treasures. These treasures are kept in a concrete, fireproof building built in imitation of the *azekura* treasuries of the past. The building contains a number of important treasures:

Kichijo-ten portrait   A rare example of a Japanese painting from the Nara period (710–794), the Kichijo-ten portrait is done in oil on linen. Originally a Hindu goddess, in Japan Kichijo-ten became associated with good fortune, beauty, happiness, peace, and learning. She is said to have been modeled after the Empress Komyo, the gentle wife of the Emperor Shomu who contributed the emperor's treasures to the Todai-ji Shoso-in after his death— or modeled after the famous Yang Kue-fei, the favorite mistress of the Chinese Emperor Ming Huang (713–755). In either case,

Kichijo-ten reflects the Tang canon of beauty—plump and matronly of figure; the gown is in the early Nara (c. 710) style of dress.

Jion Taishi portrait   A colored portrait on silk of the founder (632–682) of the Hosso sect of Buddhism. From the late Heian period (1086–1185), it is a delightful portrait of the seated priest in his bright yellow robe and vermilion surplice.

Small stupas   A portion of the 100,000 small, wooden stupas given to each of ten major temples by the Empress Koken/Shotoku in 764 for the sake of the souls of soldiers fallen on behalf of the government during an insurrection. They contain the first extant printed prayers, a milestone in printing history.

Other treasures   Various sculptures of Buddhas and bodhisattvas, and the Shinto images from the Inari and Hachiman shrines, are on view in different years. Ancient scrolls and other items of a religious nature are rotated on view with each year's showing of temple treasures.

SANZO-IN

To the north of the Yakushi-ji main complex, along the road which parallels the railway line north toward the Toshodai-ji temple is the new Sanzo-in. This recent complex represents an ambitious goal of Abbot Takeda, and it came about through the unlikely incident of the Cultural Revolution in China after the Second World War. The headquarters of the Hosso sect of Buddhism has always been in China, and it was one of the first forms of Buddhism to arrive in Japan. Under the Chinese Cultural Revolution, all forms of religion in China were put in peril, and thus Abbot Takeda determined to develop the Yakushi-ji as the head temple of Hosso Buddhism.

Fortunately for the abbot's desire, relics of one of the founding monks of Hosso Buddhism, Genjo Sanzo (Hsuan-tsang), had been brought to the Yakushi-ji in the 1940s during the Japanese invasion of China, long before the Cultural Revolution began. Thus the abbot has had a secondary temple complex created to the north of the main Yakushi-ji temple grounds. It has a central gate and a surrounding Kairo or corridor centered on an octagonal building which houses the relics of the founder and a life-sized representation of this saint. In addition, a picture hall depicting the Silk Road along which Sanzo brought sutras from India to China, with a ceiling painted to represent the heavens, lies behind the octagonal structure thereby closing the precinct on the north. Two sutra buildings housing one million small wooden stupas, each with a copy of the *Heart Sutra* created by the devotees of the sect, complete the new precincts.

TOSHODAI-JI

When the Emperor Shomu sent priestly emissaries to China in 735 to seek out a Chinese Buddhist priest who was authorized to ordain individuals into the Buddhist priesthood (a task which took them ten years), he had in mind the enhancement of the religious knowledge and life of the monks at all Nara temples. He envisioned a properly trained clergy who would forward Buddhist teachings and who could put the state under the protection of the Buddha.

The Emperor Shomu never dreamed that the priest who eventually came to Japan would, under Shomu's successor, decide that the clergy of the Todai-ji and other Nara temples were too involved in worldy pursuits to benefit from his teachings. Nor could he conceive that that priest, Ganjin (688–763), would abandon the Todai-ji to create his own temple with his own Chinese priests so as to best serve the Buddha and to offer Japan an example of what a Buddhist monastery/temple and the faith that inspired it should be like. This, of course, is what did occur, for Ganjin prevailed upon the Empress Koken/Shotoku in 759 to permit him to create the Toshodai-ji in southwest Heijo-kyo (Nara) not too far from the Yakushi-ji.

The Toshodai-ji can be reached either directly by bus 63 to the temple, as was indicated for the Yakushi-ji, or if the train is taken to Nishi-no-kyo Station one walks east from the station and then north on the first road on the left and thus to the Toshodai-ji entrance; if bus 52 is taken, one descends at the Toshodai-ji bus stop on the highway (the stop is announced in English on the bus loudspeaker) and then walks to the west to the temple entrance.

Despite the vicissitudes of time, five buildings of the early Toshodai-ji complex still survive: the great Kondo or main hall, the Kodo or lecture hall (which originally was a building in the imperial palace complex), the Kyozo or sutra storehouse, and the two *azekura* Hozo or treasuries. Thus the Toshodai-ji is unusual in that it has retained more eighth-century structures than most temples of this early period.

The Nandai-mon, the great south gate, is the entry point to the temple grounds, a gate which was reconstructed in 1963 on the 1,200 anniversary of Ganjin's death. It leads to the Kondo which was once entered through the Chu-mon or central gate and was surrounded by the Kairo (the corridors around the main buildings), units no longer in existence.

KONDO

The Kondo, the golden hall, is important both architecturally and for the fact that it is the only eighth-century Kondo of its type still standing. Its architecture is interesting since each of its seven bays grows slightly narrower as they move away from the middle bay, thus giving visual importance to the central bay in which, when the Kondo doors are open, one can see the huge image of Vairocana Buddha. The variance in the size of the bays was not only for aesthetic reasons but for practical engineering needs as well. The downward thrust or pressure of the gigantic roof is strongest at the building's corners, and thus the end bays are narrower so their columns can help to offset the thrust of the roof. The doors and windows of the front of the building are set back by one bay, thereby providing a portico under the roof, and some see in this an influence from Greek architecture as it crossed to India and thus to China. An additional possible influence from classical Greece can be observed in the entasis (the swelling in the middle) of the columns of the bays.

The Buddha and his accompanying bodhisattvas at either of his sides are so situated that they may be seen through each of the three central doorways. There was a purpose for so siting them: in the early days of Buddhism in Japan, one worshipped from outside the building since the hall was the realm of the Buddha and admission to this inner sanctum was not permitted to the mass of the people. Thus each of the images could be seen from a respectful distance, thereby adding to the awe in which they were held.

Ganjin's Chinese artist associates were responsible for the creation of the various images in the Kondo as well as for the interior decoration of the structure. The setting for the images was enhanced by the architecture and decoration of the interior of the Kondo. Above the images is a coved or latticed ceiling which still retains its floral designs, even though these paintings are badly faded after more than a millenium. The interior walls of the hall were once covered with two thousand pictures of Sakyamuni, the historic Buddha, now, unhappily, all faded from sight.

The hollow, dry-lacquer main image of the Vairocana Buddha is a 10.8-foot seated image which rests upon an 8.4-foot lotus pedestal. Behind the image, the huge aureole retains 864 of the one thousand small Buddhas which enrich it. To the right of the main image is an eighteen-foot-tall One-Thousand-Arm Kannon with 953 of its hands still intact. According to legend, the image was created by a heavenly sculptor, in contradistinction to the Vairocana Buddha which was created by one of Ganjin's Chinese artists. For ten days, according to the story, the Kondo was enshrouded in a mist, and, when the air cleared, the statue stood in place, miraculously conceived and created. Alas, despite its heavenly attributes, the image unfortunately was toppled from the upright in an 1184 earthquake, but it was restored, this time by human hands.

To the left of the Buddha is a twelve-foot-tall Yakushi Nyorai, also created in the dry-lacquer technique. Before the Kannon and the Yakushi stand a Bon-ten and a Taishaku-ten, each 5.6 feet tall and each created from a single block of wood. On guard at the four corners of the image platform are the Shitenno, the Four Guardian Kings, unusual in that they do not stand on demons whom they are trampling—as is their usual custom.

KODO

Directly behind the Kondo is the Kodo, the temple lecture hall where the abbot lectures to and questions the temple monks so as to deepen their understanding of Buddhism. This building is rather remarkable in that it was built in the year 710 as the Chodo-in (morning assembly hall) of the main precinct of the Heijo Imperial Palace. It was a gift from the Empress Koken/Shotoku in 759 and was disassembled and moved to the temple grounds where it was reconstructed for monastic purposes. It is 110.8 feet in length, and it provides an interesting contrast to the Kondo in that its long, low nature reflects Japanese tastes rather than the Tang Chinese architectural style which Ganjin's Chinese craftsmen used in creating the Kondo.

The quiet exterior of the Kodo belies the brightness of its interior with its vermilion-colored wood and its white plaster. The main, gilded image is a 5.2-foot Miroku, the Buddha of the Future, seated on a lotus with a huge gilded aureole rising 13.8 feet behind it. This Miroku from the 1200–1300s has a Jikoku-ten and a Zocho-ten, two of the Four Guardian Kings (Shitenno), on either side of it. Two ebony lecterns stand to the front left and right of the Miroku while benches line the sides of the hall for use by the monks during lecture periods. The other images which once filled the building are now in the new treasury, the better to preserve them against possible fires or earthquakes.

SHORO AND KORO

Between and to the west of the Kondo and the Kodo is the Shoro, the temple bell tower, with a bronze bell of the Heian period (794–1185) while to the east of the two main halls is the Koro or drum tower. The Koro is also called the Shari-den, the hall of relics, since three thousand grams of the Buddha's ashes, allegedly brought from China by Ganjin, were deposited here.

RAIDO

To the east of the Kondo and the Kodo is a long building running north and south, and it combines the Higashi-muro (east dormitory) and the Raido (worship hall), the latter of which is oriented to the Koro so that the ashes of the Buddha can be properly venerated.

The Raido houses at its center an image of the Shaka Nyorai in a black lacquer case, an image of Shotoku Taishi on its west, and an image of the Emperor Shomu on the east. The Shaka is a 1251 copy of the famed wooden sculpture from China in the Seiryo-ji temple in Kyoto. The Seiryo-ji Shaka was copied for a number of temples in the thirteenth century because of a rumor which spread throughout Japan in the 1200s. The year 1185 had seen the Taira-Minamoto wars and the fall of the Taira clan as the civil rulers over Japan. It marked the beginning of the Kamakura military government which removed the seat of governance from Kyoto to Kamakura and ended direct rule by the emperor. There had been warfare and civil unrest, and the times were most unsettled.

The story became widespread that the Shaka image in the Seiryo-ji, an image which had originally been brought from China, was so concerned over the situation in Japan that it was considering returning to China. Thus a number of copies were commissioned by temples and individuals who felt that the image must be preserved, should it carry out its reputed threat.

KAIDAN

A number of important units range across the northern sector of the temple on the raised ground behind the Kodo. At the western edge to the rear of the temple grounds is the Kaidan, the platform (*dan*) on which the precepts (*kai*) of Buddhism are imparted during the ordination service. Originally set up before the Daibutsuden at the Todai-ji, Ganjin created his Kaidan in his own temple when he moved here. This raised, three-tiered stone platform, erected upon earth from the sacred Mt. Wu-tai Shan of China, has a stupa in its middle. (The present structure is a thirteenth-century rebuilding.) The platform will eventually be enclosed within a building, as was the original intent.

MIEDO

In the north-central portion of the grounds is the Miedo, the founder's hall. This 1650 building was originally the imperial chamber of a sub-temple of the Kofuku-ji, but it was moved here in 1964 to house the famed colored, dry-lacquer image of Ganjin. This 2.6-foot seated image of Ganjin was created in 763, a few months before his death. (One legend claims a monk-artist had a premonition of Ganjin's death and thus created this statue from life on the day before the great priest died.) It shows him seated in meditation, his blind eyes closed, the essence of repose and tranquility. Each year on June 6, the anniversary of Ganjin's death, the doors of the Miedo are opened so the public may view this venerable statue. Another delightful tradition is realized in autumn on the night of the full moon in September when ceremonial tea is served to Ganjin's image while at the Kondo candle light is offered to the Vairocana Buddha, the Kannon, and the Yakushi images.

GANJIN'S GRAVE

To the east of the Miedo, in a wooded area reached across a bridge over a small pond, is Ganjin's grave marked by a small *gorinto* (stupa). The Chinese-style altar and balustrade were added in 1982 to enhance the grave site.

SHIN HOZO

As mentioned above, the Toshodai-ji still retains its two wooden *azekura*-style small treasuries. Such treasuries are hardly the most protective of ancient treasures, however, and thus a new fireproof building, the Shin Hozo, has been constructed. Reminiscent of the Shoso-in, in a sense, this modern concrete building is raised above the ground on pillars of cement. Its treasures are on view from March 20 to May 19 and from September 15 to November 6 annually, these many treasures being shown in rotation. Among them are:

Tosei-emaki Five of the famous *Tosei-emaki* scrolls (Travels to the East by the Great Priest of Tang [Ganjin]) are held by the temple. The story of the scrolls begins with the fourteen-year-old Ganjin visiting a temple and deciding to become a monk, and then it traces his life to his arrival in Japan. This is a later copy of the lost original.

Wooden Heads The treasury has three oversized heads of Buddhas and bodhisattvas from the late 700–800s which are fine examples of a carved wooden core which has then been covered with dry-lacquer.

Torso of a Buddha A polychromed, headless Buddha of the 800s which is noted for the gracefulness of its carved garment. This once lacquered and colored image formerly stood in the Kodo.

Dainichi Nyorai   A 10.8-foot seated, colored, dry-lacquer image from the 800s which once stood in the no-longer existent Dainichi-do. It is the oldest representation of the Dainichi Buddha in Japan.

Bodhisattvas   Ten images, originally in the Kodo, show the influence which China exerted upon Japanese sculpture. Instead of the slender images created prior to the late 600s, these figures are full-bodied and almost corpulent. Three such figures, each 5.6 feet tall, are most noted: the Bodhisattvas Shishiku and Shuho-o, and the Buddha Yakushi.

DAIAN-JI

One of the "Four Great Temples" of the Asuka region prior to its move to Nara in 718, the Daian-ji retained this status in its new site. Covering five city blocks by three blocks, it was a magnificent complex with two pagodas and many halls and dormitories. It was the residence of the Indian priest Bodhisena who held the central place in the Eye Opening Ceremony of the great Daibutsu image in the Todai-ji, and here he lived and taught Sanskrit until his death in 760.

The Daian-ji is located to the east of the Yakushi-ji. Since it is today a very small temple and is in the middle of a residential/commercial area and not convenient to public transportation, it is best to take a taxi to it and ask the taxi to wait—since the visit will not take long. If the taxi does not wait, one can walk due east from the temple to the main highway for bus 82 back to the center of town.

Once the capital moved from Nara to Nagaoka in 784 and thence to Kyoto ten years later, the Daian-ji quickly fell into disrepair. Fire reduced the temple to ashes in the 1200s, and its rebuilt structures were damaged in a 1449 earthquake. It never regained its earlier status, and by 1600 there was but one small building left with its images scattered outside the building.

TREASURE HALL

Today the Daian-ji is visited primarily at the time of year when its concrete, fireproof treasury is open to the public between October 10 and November 10. The treasury holds nine wooden images which are among the noted statues of the 700s. These include a Fukukensaku Kannon with eight arms; a Yoryu Kannon with its mouth open, an image often reproduced in art and guide books; a Sho Kannon; a Senju (One-thousand Arm) Kannon; and two of the temple's four Shitenno. Among the artifacts on view which have been found in the precincts are an interesting demon end-tile and other archeological remains. A colorful mandala hangs on the rear wall of the hall while a model of the original Daian-ji gives an idea of the tremendous size and wealth once enjoyed by this temple. Other than the October 10 to November 10 period, the temple could otherwise be bypassed since its very few modern buildings are not of note.

TOUR

 5

Heijo Palace
Hokke-ji · Futai-ji
Kombu-in
Hannya-ji

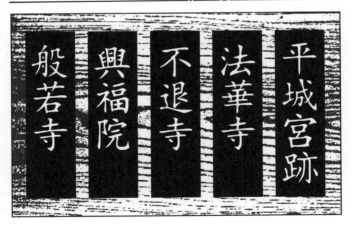

T HE NORTHERN sector of Heijo-kyo (Nara) was an aristocratic area. Not only was the imperial palace in this portion of the city, but the mansions of the nobles ran along the foot of the range of hills to the east of the palace above Ichijo-dori (First Avenue). The palace itself, under the Chinese city plan exemplified in Sian, was located in the north-central portion of Heijo-kyo with the great Suzaku-oji (Red Sparrow Boulevard) extending to the south from the palace grounds dividing the city into a left and a right sector. Inevitably, however, the Kofuku-ji temple and the Kasuga Shrine of the Fujiwaras (in what had come to be known as the "Outer Capital"), and then the creation of the Emperor Shomu's Todai-ji temple to the east of the original plan, exerted a pull on the city toward the hills to the east of the town.

With the move of the capital to Nagaoka in 784, and then to Kyoto ten years later, the Heijo-kyu palace disappeared. Some of its structures were taken down and moved to Nagaoka, and the site of the palace was not only abandoned but even its location was forgotten with time. In the last one hundred years, however, a successful attempt has been made to save the area as part of the national heritage, and archeological task forces have uncovered a great deal of material concerned with the imperial palace. Parts of the palace buildings have been re-established at their ground level, and a fine museum, the Shiryokan, has been created at the western edge of the old palace grounds. In it are housed some of the many fascinating artifacts which have been excavated.

To the west of the palace grounds lies the town of Yamato Saidai-ji with its modern shopping district and its railway station and junction of rail lines which connect Kyoto, Osaka, Nara, and Kashihara. The Akishino-dera temple, the last temple built in Nara times in the former capital, and the Saidai-ji temple, created by the Empress Koken/Shotoku out of her passion for the monk Dokyo, still stand, albeit the latter has suffered greatly with the passage of the centuries.

To the east of the palace lies the Hokke-ji temple, created originally from the mansion of Fujiwara-no-Fuhito and meant in the time of the Emperor Shomu and the Empress Komyo to be the head nunnery of all such establishments in Japan. The Hokke-ji became the residence of the Empress Komyo in her last years after she had taken religious orders, and here she cared for the sick, the elderly, and the infirm. Further to the east is the Futai-ji, once known as the Kaya Palace, a temple associated with the Emperor Heizei in the early 800s, an abdicated emperor who wished (unsuccessfully) to regain the throne and to return the capital from Kyoto to Nara. His wife and her brother were involved with him in a plot to overthrow his brother, the Emperor Saga, who had succeeded him—a failed intrigue for which his wife and her brother paid with their lives. Beyond the Futai-ji on a hillside above the city is the Kombu-in, a charming nunnery founded by a Fujiwara minister and which has a garden said to have been designed by a student of the noted seventeenth-century landscape designer Kobori Enshu.

Finally, the tombs of the Emperor Shomu and the Empress Komyo are preserved in a park toward the end of Ichijo-dori at the banks of the small Saho River, just a few streets before the Tegai-mon gateway to the Todai-ji temple. To the north of these tombs and the main portion of the city is the Hannya-ji, a temple with a huge stone pagoda surrounded by a rampant planting of cosmos. (Dreamland, a pale, small reflection of a 1960s copy of Disneyland, exists to the north of the city also. It can best be ignored since it adds little to the historic importance or attractiveness of Nara!)

We can begin this tour with the former imperial palace and then work our way east to the Hannya-ji, leaving the Akishino-dera and the Saidai-ji on the west and the Joruri-ji on the northeast to another tour. We begin by taking bus 12, 13, or 14 from the bus terminal at Noborioji or bus 12 from the Saidai-ji Kintetsu Railway Station (north side), or by taking a taxi to the palace site.

HEIJO PALACE

The Heijo Palace site has been under excavation since 1958, and knowledge not only of the palace and of the administrative quarters of the 700s has increased greatly, but artifacts which have been unearthed have thrown new light on the living and social conditions of that era. In many ways, it is best to begin a visit to the former palace area at the Shiryokan, the main palace site museum, since the dioramas and models, as well as the findings of the excavations and of research, place the palace and its times in a proper context.

SHIRYOKAN

The museum of the Heijo Palace is in a modern building which is adjacent to the laboratories and storage areas of the Cultural Research Institute where artifacts are treated and preserved after they have been excavated. The entry hall of the museum contains an information desk and a literature sales counter, the walls of the hall holding a series of photo-mural displays of the city of Nara and of the ancient palace area. Excellent overlays of the palace grounds on photo maps of Nara city indicate the extent of the one-time governmental center of early Japan.

The exhibition halls display models of buildings of the palace and government offices as well as a full display of the many artifacts which have been unearthed. These include clay vessels for ritual and kitchen use, wooden stupas, wooden figures with jointed arms and legs, spools and spindles for textile making, beads, needles, wooden clogs, and various metal objects ranging from ritual knives to locks and bells. There is even a wooden passport for a traveler to the capital from Omi Province (present-day Shiga Prefecture).

PALACE SITE

The public bus leaves one at the northern side of the palace grounds, but the palace would originally have been approached from the south along the broad, willow-tree-lined Suzaku-oji which ran from the southern edge of the capital to the imperial precincts at the boulevard's northern terminus. The gate to the palace grounds was impressive, since it was larger than the Nandai-mon at the Todai-ji temple today, and it was but one of twelve gates which pierced the palace walls which encompassed the entire site. Within these perimeter walls, palace buildings were surrounded by their own walls, and some of these walls have been reconstructed in the restored areas.

Archeological exploration, which began in 1958 and has now uncovered some twenty-five percent of the palace site, has ascertained that there were two palace sites parallel to each other at various times, and the reason for these alternate sites is still not clear to scholars. The eastern site has been partially restored so as

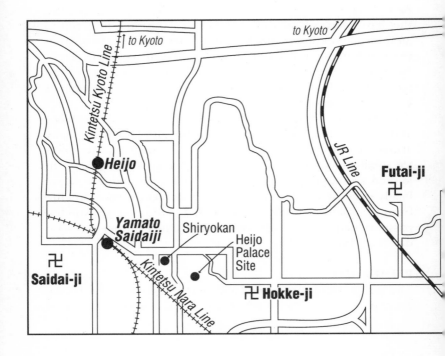

to present an idea of the layout of the original buildings. Grass and gravel indicate where walls had been, while clipped evergreens have been planted to show where the pillars of buildings once stood. The raised platform of the Daigokuden, the Imperial Council Hall, has been re-established in masonry with the bases for its pillars indicated. From its elevation there is an excellent view over the palace grounds and of the Yamato Plain stretching to the south between the eastern and western range of mountains on either side of Nara.

NORTHEAST MUSEUM
Three buildings which constitute a "junior museum" are located in the northeast sector of the grounds. Here excavation pits have been preserved to illustrate what archeologists find in the nature

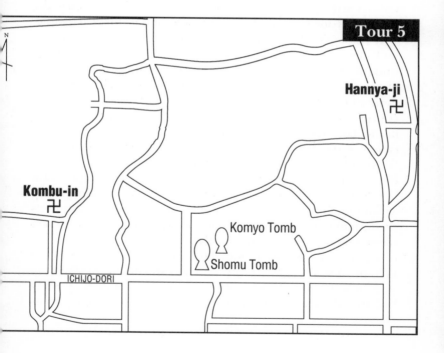

of depressions and holes which once held the posts of buildings. Models of buildings, walls, and gates show the structures which formerly adorned the palace grounds.

The palace site is an interesting one to wander about, and there is usually one sector which is undergoing current archeological search. Most important, however, is the previously mentioned palace museum which pulls together the findings of the archeologists and presents a more complete view of the palace and governmental buildings and what life in the eighth century would have been like.

HOKKE-JI

Bus 12 from the Heijo Palace can take one to the Hokke-ji-mae bus stop which is one street to the east of the temple. Or, one can walk from the palace bus stop for two streets to the east, two to the south, and one street to the east to arrive at the Hokke-ji temple.

If Nara were fortunate in having the Emperor Shomu who built the magnificent Todai-ji and tried his best to spread the Buddhist faith throughout Japan, it was equally fortunate in that Shomu's consort was the gentle Empress Komyo. Komyo was a devoted Buddhist, not merely in the ritualistic sense but in her concern for the well-being of all sentient beings. In many ways, particularly where charity was concerned, she was the personification of the essence of the teachings of the Buddha and the bodhisattvas. To many individuals of her time, she seemed the reincarnation of Kannon, the Bodhisattva of Mercy, and, with her devotion to the welfare of others, these public feelings were well founded. Of all of her many good works and the institutions she founded, the Hokke-ji remains today as one of the primary reminders of the life of this saintly woman.

The Empress Komyo founded the Hokke-ji nunnery in 741 so as to provide a religious profession and an equality of status for women within the Buddhist faith, a concern not held by many Buddhist theologians and priests in eighth-century Japan. It was here that she retired after she and Shomu abdicated, each to take up the religious life. As the Todai-ji was established as the head temple for all provincial monasteries in Japan, so the Hokke-ji served as the head temple for the nation's nunneries. The original buildings of this nunnery had been the mansion of Komyo's father, the great Fujiwara-no-Fuhito who had established the capital in Nara and who had been the first minister of the imperial rulers. In the mansion's new incarnation as a nunnery, it was here in the bathhouse that the empress labored along with the nuns in washing the sick, succoring the poor and elderly, and ministering to all in need—as a Buddhist saint should.

As with many religious institutions, the nunnery's physical buildings declined when the capital departed Nara, but much of the small complex was restored during the Momoyama period (1568–1615). Once the grounds were far more extensive than they are now, and pagodas formerly stood to the south beyond the present road before the compound. Today the main entrance to the smaller temple precincts is through the south gate or Nan-mon, and within the walls surrounding the nunnery are a Momoyama period Shoro (belfry) in drum style with a "skirt" base from 1601, a pond, and a large stone lantern which lies before the Hondo (main hall).

HONDO

The present Hondo was constructed at the end of the 1500s by Yodogimi, the wife of Toyotomi Hideyoshi, the civil ruler of the day, and its prize possession is a 3.3-foot-tall Juichimen Kannon (Eleven-Headed Kannon) carved from a single block of camphor wood which stands within a richly lacquered black cabinet. Until the Meiji period (1868–1912) the image was a hidden image, but today its case is open from March 20 to April 7, from June 6 to 8, and from October 25 to November 8.

Legend recounts that the statue was carved from life by a sculptor from India who had the empress herself as his model.

(Since the image is from the 800s or later, this is probably an apocryphal tale.) Another tradition claims that an Indian king dreamed that he would find a living bodhisattva in Japan (the Empress Komyo). Unable to leave his throne, he sent a sculptor to create an image of this living bodhisattva and to bring the sculpture back to India. The artist is said to have obtained but a fleeting glimpse of the empress, but from this glimpse he carved two statues, one of which is in the nunnery and the other of which is said to have been taken to India. The grace, the charm, and the attractiveness of the image could lead one to accept the legend that it is a true likeness of the empress, the living bodhisattva of the eighth century.

Along the side walls of the Hondo are other Buddhist images. Three large heads are mounted at the left rear, remains of images from the 700s or 800s. One is the head of the Buddha, two feet tall and covered with lacquer and gold leaf. The other two of similar size are of Bonten and Taishakuten. To the right front of the hall are additional images of an Eleven-Headed Kannon, a Fudo Myo-o, and an Aizen Myo-o on a lion. At the rear of the hall are representations of Jizo, Fudo, and Miroku.

The main image, in its own black lacquered case in the central altar area, is that of the Eleven-Headed Kannon, supposedly of Komyo herself, protected by the four Shitenno Kings, one at each corner of the altar platform. To its left, at the entrance to the hall, behind the entry desk, one can often see a nun at work, continuing the tradition said to have been begun by Komyo herself of creating tiny images of spotted white dogs from the ashes of the incense burned before the religious images in the hall. These charms are said to help women in childbirth and in illness, and they are much in demand and thus they sell out early most mornings.

KARABURO

To the west of the Hondo is a modern building commemorating the Empress Komyo and the bathhouse in which she once cared for the elderly and the ill. Today it serves primarily as an exhibition hall for exhibits concerned with the nunnery, Buddhism, and the nunnery's beloved empress.

GARDENS AND PRIVATE BUILDINGS

To the east of the Hondo is an opening in the inner temple wall, and this leads into the grounds of the private residence and gardens of the nuns. From May 1 to May 15 and again from October 10 to November 10, this private portion of the nunnery is open to the public. The present living quarters of the compound once formed a part of the imperial palace in Kyoto, a gift to the nunnery in the Edo period (1615–1868). A famous garden about the pond within these private quarters reflects the Momoyama style (1568–1615) which was employed in the gardens of Kyoto at that time. The garden and the pond lie behind the Hondo and are viewed from one of the tatami-matted rooms of the nunnery residence.

Within the private section to the east of the entry path into the nunnery grounds and gardens is a tea house with a thatched roof, reminiscent of an attractive, small farmhouse. Beyond these private gardens, further to the east (in an area which can also be reached from the main precincts through an opening in the wall beyond the entry gate to the Hokke-ji) is a bathhouse. While not the original of the empress' time, it recalls the legend that when the magnificent Todai-ji Daibutsuden was completed, the empress vowed to wash one thousand indigent or aged persons in gratitude to the Buddha for the succesful dedication of that great temple. She washed 999 individuals, and the last one, a leper, upon the completion of her task, revealed himself to be a manifestation of the divine.

FUTAI-JI

Bus 12, 13, or 14 from the Hokke-ji-mae bus stop will take one to the east along Ichijo-dori (First Avenue) to the Futai-ji-guchi bus stop just across the main north-south highway (National Route 24). The first street to the north of Ichijo-dori after crossing the main highway leads to the Futai-ji, crossing the railroad tracks en route.

A quiet, small temple, away from the bustle of the city, the Futai-ji seems an unlikely place for a plot against the ruling emperor, or, in time, the residence of one of the ninth century's greatest rakes—an era when many aspired to (and often succeeded in) achieving that status. Nor would one suspect that, despite the dictates of the Meiji period (1868–1912) government, a combination of Buddhism and Shintoism would remain visible within the small Hondo of the temple.

Today's Futai-ji was at one time (810–824) the detached Kaya Palace of the retired Emperor Heizei. The emperor had an affection for Nara, and he had tried unsuccessfully to have the capital returned to Nara from Kyoto. Thwarted in his desires, he abdicated in 809 and built his retirement mansion here at the foot of Kurogamiyama hill, a former area of mansions of the aristocracy of Nara in its great days. He soon regretted having given up power, and with his wife and her brother (Fujiwara-no-Nakanari), he plotted to overthrow the Emperor Saga, his brother, to whom he had abdicated the throne. Emperor Saga acted quickly, and the ensuing revolt was quickly put down. As a result, Heizei's wife took poison, and her brother was put to death. The ex-Emperor Heizei and his oldest son were forced to shave their heads and to become monks, and Heizei spent the last fourteen years of his life in his Nara palace now turned into a monastic retreat. The son eventually went on a pilgrimage to India but was presumed lost en route since he never returned.

After Heizei's death, the mansion belonged to another of his sons, Abe-Shin-o, and then to his grandson Ariwara-no-Narihira (823–880). Narihira was renowned in his own day as a poet and as a rake. His *Tales of Ise* are primarily autobiographical and are really love poems concerned with Narihira's romantic exploits which are best summed up in his own words: "It is a general rule in this world that some men love some women but not others. Narihira did not make such distinctions." It was this courtier and grandson of the former Emperor Heizei who turned the mansion into a temple in 847 upon an imperial order. Even courtly love, he sadly found, comes to an end, and, being ill and fearful he might die, he wrote a brief poem:

> That it is a road
> Which someday we all must travel
> I had heard before.
> Yet I never expected
> To take it so soon myself.

TAHO-TO

The temple prospered for a few years before a decline set in, and its history is unspectacular thereafter; its present buildings represent a 1930 restoration. Past the Nan-mon (south gate) of 1317, one enters a small courtyard with shrubs, bushes, cosmos, roses, and chrysanthemums. To the right is a pond, and beyond it is the lower level of the Taho-to, the remains of a one-time, two-story pagoda with a Dainichi Nyorai image of the Buddha of the Great Sun within it. The ceiling of the Taho-to is decorated with elaborately colored floral and arabesque designs which have suffered with the passage of time. The Taho-to is, unfortunately, not generally open to the public.

HONDO

At the end of the path through the courtyard garden, a tall stone lantern stands before the Hondo (main hall). The exterior of the building is a faded red, but the interior is brilliant in its vermilion and white colors. There are a number of Myo-o figures within the central area, an indication that the Futai-ji became a Shingon temple in time since these are favored deities of that sect of Buddhism. The Hondo also contains a figure of Abe-Shin-o, the father of Narihira and a son of the Emperor Heizei.

The rear portion of the Hondo is divided into three sections: the left unit holds the image of Abe-Shin-o; the central portion contains the main image, a 6.3-foot Sho Kannon in wood with a large ribbon tied in a bow in its hair on either side of its head, the length of the ribbon falling over each shoulder. A Jizo image stands before the Kannon to its right while a Fudo is in front to its left. The four other images, one in each corner, are interesting since they represent the Esoteric (Mikkyo) form of Buddhism which was popularized as Shingon Buddhism by Kobo Daishi (Kukai) after the year 800. A facet of late Indian Tantric Buddhism, these deities were originally the personification of magic formulae. Terrifying in appearance, they are really benevolent beings whose fearful visages are meant to frighten away evil. In the left front is Dai Itoku with his six arms and legs, seated on an ox; in the rear behind him is a multi-arm Myo-o while another Myo-o is to the right front and to the right rear corners.

The third or right-hand section of the three sectors is unusual since this temple retains a Shinto shrine within its main hall. Shinto shrines and Buddhist temples were separated in the anti-Buddhist crusade of State Shinto after 1870, but the Futai-ji has kept its shrine with its altar and hanging which came from Ise. No doubt it is the connection with the great Shinto shrine at Ise to which Abe-Shin-o made a pilgrimage and returned with the banner in the Hondo which saved the shrine from removal. The walls of the area are painted white, and behind the altar is a painted red disc representing the sun.

An opening in the garden west wall leads to a building with a tatami-floored room where tea may be obtained as well as postcards of the temple. Just to the north of the tea room in the garden is an empty fifth-century stone coffin.

KOMBU-IN

Bus 12, 13, or 14 can be taken three stops (eleven streets) further along Ichijo-dori to the east to a street which leads north to the walls about the Kombu-in. The nunnery is on the lower slopes of Kurogamiyama hill, just below the modern Dreamland Amusement Park.

Nestled against the hillside, the Kombu-in is one of the more delightful temple complexes of Nara, for its gardens and its architecture complement the wooded hillside and offer a pleasant view of the mountains to the southwest. (Unfortunately, a view directly to the south and to the west brings the sprawl of modern Nara into view!) Its Hondo with its use of gold leaf and colored decoration is equally striking.

The Kombu-in was originally built in 771 at the request of Fujiwara-no-Momokawa, a state minister, and tradition claims that it was moved to its present location in 1665. Momokawa was noted for his probity after the scandalous reigns of the Empress Koken/Shotoku. When she died, it was agreed by the court nobles that no woman would serve as ruler again (a tradition not broken until the seventeenth century) lest she be influenced by a handsome priest, as had happened with the late empress. Thus an elderly emperor was chosen as an interim ruler. Shortly before his death, he decided to appoint a daughter by his favorite concubine as empress. Momokawa not only objected, but he stood outside the palace gates for forty days in protest—until the emperor gave in and appointed his oldest son as his successor. That emperor, Kammu, was to move the capital from Nara in 784 to rid the court of priestly interference.

An impressive main gateway with a sliding door on its left side provides an entry to the grounds. The main path to the Hondo (main hall) is to the right, three tiers of steps leading to a second gate. There a striking vista appears: a long, broad flight of stone steps with two tall stone lanterns at the top flanking the Hondo with its heavy tiled roof lie before one. At the head of the steps, a large Shoro (belfry) on the right holds the nunnery's huge temple bell while to the left of the Hondo a covered, arched bridge leads to a covered walk which descends to and terminates at the nuns' residence.

HONDO

The interior of the Hondo is more colorful than most temples in Nara. Its upright posts are covered with gold leaf and are painted in bright colors in geometric designs at their upper portions, even the frog-leg supports and horizontal beams are decorated with brilliant color. The main Amida image and his bodhisattvas are covered with gold leaf, and the ceiling over each image has a flat, golden lotus with gold lacework metal hangings in a circlet over each figure. The wall behind the images is covered with paintings done in gold leaf, and the effect of the gold against the black lacquered furniture and the brown wooden ceiling is most striking.

Outside, to the left of the Hondo, an arched bridge crosses an arm of a small pond and leads to a covered walkway which heads down to the convent residence and its gateway, a gateway which is closed to the public. From this gateway one can look back up the hillside one has descended to a garden of azaleas and other bushes, the moss-covered ground, and a small stream descending from the pond above. This most pleasant garden is said to be the one which was created by the student of Kobori Enshu.

Behind the Hondo is the mausoleum (Daiyu-in) of Shogun Tokugawa Hidetada (1579–1632), the son of Tokugawa Ieyasu and the second of the Tokugawa shoguns.

TOMBS OF EMPEROR SHOMU AND EMPRESS KOMYO

Continuing some eleven more streets to the east along Ichijo-dori, one comes to a park just before the small Saho River (more a brook than a river at this point). Within the park-like area are the graves of the emperor and empress who saw to the development of some of the major temples of Nara in the mid-eighth century as well as being responsible for the receipt by the Todai-ji's Shoso-in of the ten thousand rare and exquisite items owned by the emperor, which can periodically still be seen each late autumn at the Nara National Museum. As was the Buddhist custom, the bodies of Shomu and Komyo were cremated after their death, and their ashes were deposited in separate but adjacent graves to the north of the Saho River and within view of the great roof of the Daibutsuden of the Todai-ji, a temple which Shomu had brought into being.

A long graveled path leads from Ichijo-dori to a tree-covered hillside. The lane leading straight back from the street ends at a stone-fenced enclosure with a stone torii, a burial place of great simplicity and dignity. Here lie the ashes of the Emperor Shomu (died 756). Where the path branches to the right, a similar stone-fenced enclosure leads to the grave of the Empress Komyo (died 760). The graves of these two rulers appear as they were enhanced under the government program of the late 1800s.

From the Shomu and Komyo tombs, one can continue east on Ichijo-dori to the main highway, opposite the Tegai-mon gateway to the Todai-ji grounds, and there one can take bus 82, 84, or 86 to the third bus stop, the Hannya-ji bus stop. (These buses can also be taken from the JR station or from the north side of Noborioji opposite the bus station.)

Instead, one could walk north on the highway, not forgetting to pass the Tegai-mon gate across from Ichijo-dori in case tradition holds true that walking by it cures all disease. Continuing straight ahead on the north-south highway, when the highway veers to the right, the new northbound street straight ahead will take one through a residential section of the city seldom visited by foreigners, and along the way a former leper hospital, the Kitayama Juhachiken-do, is passed.

The Kitayama Juhachiken-do (North Hill Eighteen Bay Hall) was created by the priest Ninsho (1217–1303) in the 1200s to house and care for victims of leprosy. A long building of eighteen bays, it was compartmented for the better care of its residents. Rebuilt between 1661 to 1673 when it was moved to its present location, it was in use until the nineteenth century. The building is now abandoned and is not open to the public, but it is of interest both historically and architecturally, and it is on the right as one ascends the slight slope toward the Hannya-ji temple.

HANNYA-JI

In the great days of Heijo-kyo (Nara), the Hannya-ji site was far beyond the city limits, and it served as an execution ground as well as a burial site. Documentation indicates that the Hannya-ji temple was in existence by 712, but the date of its founding is uncertain. It was burned to the ground by Taira-no-Shigehira and his troops when they destroyed Nara in 1180, but it was rebuilt ten years later. After the defeat of the Taira, Shigehira was turned over to the monks of Nara, and their fury over the destruction of their temples overcame the Buddhist precept against the taking of life—a precept warrior-monks usually ignored. Shigehira was executed at the Hannya-ji area execution ground, and his head was displayed at the site of the temple.

As was so often the case with temples, fires continued to obliterate the Hannya-ji, and thus its present buildings date from the 1600s. The large and impressive Ro-mon (Tower Gate) in Chinese style, however, survives from the 1200s, and through it can be seen the huge thirteen-tiered stone pagoda of 1261. The temple grounds are entered through a modern entryway just to the north of the two-story Ro-mon, and beyond the entry and around the Hondo are rows of fascinating votive stones with multi-arm Kannon in relief on their surface. These attractive units are considered to be among the finest in Japan, and in late summer they are partially hidden by the multitude of cosmos which grow in profusion in the temple grounds.

The major element in the temple precincts is the thirteen-tiered stone pagoda from 1261 which rises forty-nine feet into the air. It too is considered one of the finest of its kind in Japan, and thus the votive stones, the stone pagoda, the Kasotoba, and the Chinese gate are worth making the journey to this somewhat out-of-the-way temple. Temple legend claims that the Emperor Shomu had a copy of the *Dai Hannya-kyo Sutra* buried where the pagoda now stands, but the pagoda is of a later date than the emperor's time.

There are two other "pagodas" or stupas on the grounds, although they are of a different nature. These Kasatoba from 1264 are each some sixteen feet tall and are to the east of the Hondo. Kasatoba are roofed stone-posts or stupas ("roofed" in the sense that these square pillars have a capstone atop them which in turn is surmounted by two stone rings crowned with a stone "jewel"). Each of these units is inscribed with the name of the donor, a Chinese Sung artisan, as a blessing for his parents.

Within the Hondo, the altar area is divided into three sections with a wood Monju image holding a lotus in his left hand and a sword in his right. Since the *Hannya-kyo Sutra* is concerned with that true wisdom from which Enlightenment springs, and since Monju represents supreme wisdom, he is an appropriate main image for the temple. In addition, in Buddhist tradition Monju is responsible for the northeast sector of the Buddhist universe—as the Hannya-ji serves as a protecting temple to the northeast of Nara. In the Hannya-ji, Monju sits upon a golden lotus blossom which is on top of the back of a lion. A later replacement for a lost original, the image which was originally in the Kyozo-do (sutra storage hall) was created by the sculptor Kosei in 1324. This gold-leaf-covered Monju, carved from one block of wood, is 16.7 inches tall and has his hair drawn up in eight topknots signifying that Monju is the embodiment of an eight-syllable mantra (a magical syllable or spell). The large golden aureole behind Monju has a lacy perimeter of flowers and scrollwork.

Seated on a Chinese chair to Monju's left is a small figure of Binzuru, the physician who followed the Buddha Gautama. On Monju's right is a treasure chest protected with a Shinto straw rope and white paper *shimenawa;* it is a Chinese chest of Tang style, and it holds the temple's *Hannya-kyo Sutra*. The far left has a seated image of Kobo Daishi (Kukai) with a Tamon-ten and Komoku-ten guardian behind him, while to the far right is a seated Fudo, a huge halo of flames enveloping him. He is guarded by the temple's other two Shitenno, Zocho-ten and Jikoku-ten.

In the southeast corner of the grounds is the Kyozo-do (sutra storage hall); to the west of the Hondo is the temple Shoro (belfry); while to the rear of the Hondo is the treasure hall and a traditional tea room. The treasure hall is open from April 29 to May 10 and from October 26 to November 10, but its treasures do not bear comparison with those in other Nara temples.

TOUR

Shin Yakushi-ji
Gango-ji
Jurin-in
Byakugo-ji

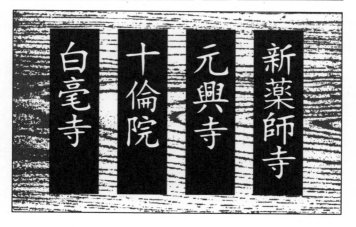

T OUR 4 discussed the move of three of the great temples of the Asuka region to Nara once the new capital of Heijo-kyo had been established. Of the three, the Yakushi-ji still remains, is prospering, and is gradually being returned in the twentieth century to its former glory. The Daian-ji, however, has almost disappeared, its modern, concrete treasure hall alone being of importance today. The third temple was the one with the oldest heritage, the Hoko-ji or Asuka-dera, the first Buddhist temple to be built in Japan in 588 by Soga-no-Umako, the then ruling civil leader who defeated the anti-Buddhist forces of his day and opened the door to the flourishing of Buddhism in the nation. The Hoko-ji temple followed the court to Heijo-kyo in 718, leaving its original buildings and images behind and creating a new and magnificent monastic center in southeast Nara under the new name of Gango-ji. Today it, too, has been very much diminished, but its history and its two buildings and museum are worthy of recall.

Four sites other than the Gango-ji are of note in the southeast sector of Nara. These are Zuto or Head Mound, an earthen structure of some mystery, the Shin Yakushi-ji temple with its noted circle of Buddhist statuary, the Byakugo-ji which can introduce us to the ferocious-looking Emma, the King of Hell, and the Jurin-in, a delightful small temple with a most unusual stone, cave-like altar area.

ZUTO

The city circular bus route to the Wariishi-cho bus stop to the south of the park around the Kasuga Shrine leaves one at a modern apartment house. Behind it, within a fence, is the small hill called Zuto.

The purpose of Zuto (Head Mound), the high mound in eastern Nara, is one of those debatable matters. It is thought by some that it was once a portion of the Shin Yakushi-ji temple grounds, and one opinion holds that it was the site of the Shin Yakushi-ji pagoda, a fairly unlikely proposal since it would put the temple pagoda at the northern rather than the normal southern side of the temple complex. On the other hand, the mound is also said to have been built in 767 in imitation of an Indian stupa by the priest Jocchu, a disciple of Abbot Roben of the Todai-ji temple, created at the abbot's order as an offering to regain peace and to protect the nation in times of internal discord during the reigns of the Empress Koken/Shotoku.

Yet another tradition claims that this was the burial site of the priest Gembo and that the mound was constructed over Gembo's head (thus its name of Head Mound) to pacify the soul of Fujiwara-no-Hirotsugu. Hirotsugu was decapitated by an all too eager general after the failure of Hirotsugu's revolt in Kyushu after he had risen in rebellion when the court refused to remove Gembo from his religious office. Hirotsugu, as with Ganjin who left the Todai-ji in disgust with the attitudes and conduct of its clergy, demanded that the court cleanse itself of corruption by ridding the Kofuku-ji of Gembo who was not worthy of his priestly status as the head of the northern branch of the Hosso sect of Buddhism. When the court did nothing, Hirotsugu rose in revolt in Kyushu—and was executed without imperial permission by the over-eager general who had defeated the rebelling forces.

Be that as it may, Zuto is a 395-foot-tall hill of three levels with a number of stones on each level ranging from twelve to twenty inches tall, each carved in relief with a Buddha accompanied by two bodhisattvas. Five small stupas *(gorinto)* were added to the south side in the 1200s. In recent years archeologists have been examining the mound, and thus more information concerning Zuto should be available in time.

SHIN YAKUSHI-JI

One would not believe today, from its obscure location in a southeast residential area, that the Shin (new) Yakushi-ji was once a temple built on a major scale by the Empress Komyo. The temple can be reached from the Wariishi-cho bus stop of the circular bus route by walking east two streets to a street which heads south to the temple.

Constructed in 747 and dedicated to the Buddha Yakushi, the Buddha of Healing and Medicine, it was created at the request of the Empress Komyo as an offering for the curing of an eye ailment of the Emperor Shomu. Its importance can be realized by the fact that it was planned and erected by the same government bureau which was building the great Todai-ji temple at the same time. Located to the east of the capital, there are those who feel that it was so situated as to complement the Yakushi-ji temple on the western side of the city. At one time there were seven Yakushi images in the temple, but time and fire have taken their toll of all but one image. The present Hondo (main hall) is the only structure left from the eighth century, and it is thought that it originally served as the monastic refectory. It and the main hall of the Akishino-dera temple to the north of Yamato Saidai-ji Station are the only eighth-century buildings extant in Nara which have always served as temple buildings. (The Toshodai-ji Kodo originally was part of the eighth-century palace buildings and thus was not intended for worship.)

The north-south street which leads to the temple ends at a four-foot-tall pillar shaped like a woman with a baby on her back, reminiscent of an ancient *haniwa* figure, before the road turns to the right. At the corner after the turning is a very small Shinto shrine against the south wall of the temple grounds. The entrance to the Shin Yakushi-ji grounds is in the center of this southern wall, and outside of the wall to the left of this entryway is a full-scale Kagami Shinto Shrine with its torii, Haiden (offertory), Honden (spirit hall), and shrine offices.

Within the temple walls, on the right, is the two-story Shoro (belfry) of 1279 with a bell which is reputed to have once belonged to the not too distant Gango-ji temple. There are two small Shinto shrines, one to the right and one to the left of the main path, as well as a small unit containing stone images of the Buddha and bodhisattvas. A very small one-bay Jizo-do (Jizo hall) holds a stone image of Jizo while a thirteen-tiered stone pagoda stands to its south.

HONDO

A large stone lantern stands at the head of the main path just before the Hondo (main hall). The seven-bay hall has three sets of doors but no windows, and thus having a flashlight is helpful in viewing the images within the structure. (The temple has flashlights which may be borrowed, but their beam is sometimes pitifully weak.) The exterior roof should be observed before entering the Hondo since its eighth-century demon end-tiles are still retained on the roof of the hall.

The interior of the Hondo is unusual in that the altar is a circular, raised clay platform with the Yakushi Buddha in its center and with the clay images of the Juni Shinsho, the Twelve Divine Generals, around the periphery of the circle guarding the

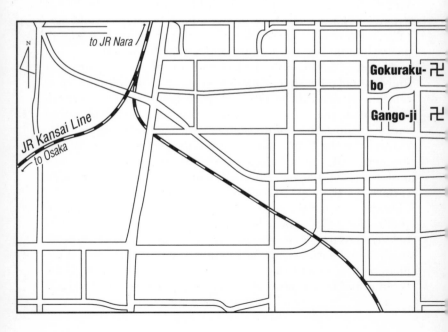

Buddha. These generals are not original to the temple, having been brought from another site, and they are considered of second quality, being somewhat stiff in pose and with armor seemingly cast from one mold. These clay figures date from 748 and their costumes have a Near-Eastern appearance. A few of the generals are among those of most interest: Basara Taisho with his ferocious look and bulging eyes, his hair standing on end; Indara Taisho with a trident and helmet; Santera Taisho with a trident; and Makoro Taisho with a hatchet. These images were once more colorful, and the faded greens, blues, and reds which can still be discerned give but a hint of the vivid figures they would once have been. The generals are said to represent the twelve vows made by Yakushi to save all sentient beings, and they serve to protect his Joruri (Eastern) Paradise.

The main image is an eighth-century seated Yakushi Nyorai, carved from one huge block of *hinoki* (Japanese cypress). This

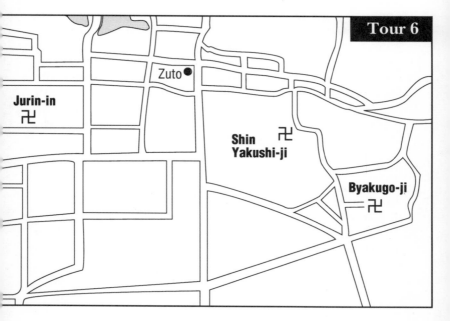

7.9-foot-tall, too-corpulent image has the full-bodied style of Tang Chinese sculptures, and in its hugeness it is not too attractive. His right hand is at his breast while in his left hand he holds the medicine pot usually associated with Yakushi. Directly behind him is a Jizo holding the *centamani* magical jewel in one hand and a bamboo staff in the other.

Images of various sizes line the rear wall: Jizos, kings, priests, ranging from eighteen inches to six feet in size. Giving the appearance of a poorly arranged storage area, these images would once have had a position of importance elsewhere in the temple's buildings when the Shin Yakushi-ji had its full complement of religious halls.

The columns supporting the Hondo roof should be noted since they end in wooden capitals, a touch which some feel reflects a Greek architectural influence which traveled the far distance of the Silk Road to Japan. These columns were once highly colored, but their flowery images are now badly faded. Thus the colored generals and the colored imagery of the columns would once have made this an exotic-appearing hall.

In the western portion of the temple grounds a doorway in the west wall leads to a bridge over a pond and to a building where tea is served on low tables on tatami mats. Of the ceremonies at the Shin Yakushi-ji, the most noted is the Shuni-e Ceremony on April 8 at 7:00 p.m. when twelve huge torches are burned while twelve priests representing the Juni Shinsho, the Twelve Divine Generals, recite from temple sutras.

GANGO-JI

Two temples are now often referred to as the Gango-ji due to the division of the original temple site, the main structures of which now lie four streets south of the staircase from the Kofuku-ji temple and south along the street on the east side of the Sarusawa Pond.

When Nara was chosen as the site of the new capital of Heijo-kyo, a number of the buildings which had existed in the early capital twenty miles to the south could be moved to their new locations since the buildings were based on a post-and-beam construction which did not use nails. It was thus possible to dismantle a building and move its parts slowly and ponderously on oxen carts to the new site where it could be re-assembled. On the other hand, with virgin forests still in abundance, new raw materials were always available for construction. In the case of the Gango-ji, its former buildings seem to have been left behind.

When the imperial capital was located in Fujiwara-kyo to the south of present-day Nara, one of the most important and the oldest temple in the Asuka region was the Hoko-ji or Asuka-dera, the first Buddhist temple built in Japan in 588 by Soga-no-Umako, the ruthless political power behind the imperial throne. When the Hoko-ji relocated to Nara in 718, it emerged as a larger, major new temple/monastery under the name of Gango-ji. The original Hoko-ji site in Asuka, however, remained as a temple with its original Buddha image, the first ever created in Japan. Today, as the Hoko-ji or Asuka-dera, what remains of that early temple and its original Buddha image may still be visited.

When the new Gango-ji was finally completed after twenty-three years of construction, it emerged as one of the Four Great Temples of Nara, a major religious unit in a new city. Its plan called for two pagodas (only one was built), a Kondo (golden hall), a Kodo (lecture hall), and a full array of Kuri (priests' quarters) for its many monks, as well as the needed Jiki-do (refectory) and other ancillary buildings.

In Nara the temple was honored by having Gyogi as one of its monks. It was he who raised funds and materials for the initial construction of the Todai-ji by preaching to all levels of men, an action at first frowned upon by the court which felt that Buddhism was only for the protection of the nobles and of the state. His desire to bring Buddhism to the common man drove him, but such a goal was not fully achieved until after the Gango-ji had lost its religious importance and much of its property.

Destroyed in the great conflagration of the southern capital in 1180, along with other temples, it was later rebuilt. With the passage of time it did not, however, answer to the needs of the mass of the people who were now accepting Buddhism, and it gradually fell into decay. A new temple, the Gokuraku-bo, was erected on a small portion of its grounds, and its two buildings and a modern treasure hall are all that remain of the one-time magnificent complex. Separated by a residential section, a small portion of the temple grounds remains to the south with the site of the original pagoda and a small temple building of a later date which still is known as the Gango-ji.

GOKURAKU-BO

The three buildings at the Gokuraku-bo today are the Hondo (main hall), the Zenshitsu or Zen-do (Zen meditation hall), and the treasure hall. The first two buildings were once a portion of the monks' quarters of the Gango-ji, but in 1244 these dormitories were made over into two buildings to serve local religious needs. The Hondo on the east has white shoji on three sides, and its main object is a Jodo (Pure Land) mandala on wood at the rear of the altar area, a Muromachi (1333–1573) copy of the original seventh-century mandala. The temple had early developed as a Jodo center for the worship of Amida and his Western Paradise as a result of a vision of the priest Chiko of the temple in a dream in which he was directed to concentrate his faith on Amida and Amida's promise to save all beings. Chiko's quarters at the temple have become the Gokuraku-bo (paradise hall) with the mandala of Amida's Western Paradise which he had seen in his vision as its center piece. Today the rear wall behind the altar with its mandala has *ihei* (memorial tablets to the dead) at either end and then in the center are some fifty images of Jizo on either side of a Kannon image.

ZENSHITSU

When the monks' eighth-century dormitory was rebuilt as two

buildings, the second and longer unit became the Zenshitsu or Zen-do. This twelve-bay building consists primarily of one long tatami-matted room with a few small rooms at its western end.

Most striking about the temple today is the arrangement of the hundreds of small memorial stones between the Zenshitsu and the treasure hall. Brought together from various areas, these Jizo images and gravestones, engraved with Buddhas or religious texts, have been arranged in rows between the two buildings. A Shinto shrine is to the east of the treasure hall among these memorial stones.

TREASURE HALL

The Treasure Hall behind the memorial stones holds images and artifacts from the Gango-ji's once greater glory. An outline of the original complex appears on a large-scale photograph of Nara, thereby showing the major land area the temple once covered. A large model of the original Gango-ji temple with its many, many buildings is also on display. A 17.4-foot-model of the one-time pagoda is a fine piece of early workmanship and indicates the impressive nature of the actual unit before it was destroyed by fire in 1859. In 1927 the thirty-three-square-foot site of the pagoda was excavated, and 118 feet underground the original jewels and coins buried beneath the pagoda's center pole were recovered after more than a millenium. The pagoda site is now in the small, modern Gango-ji local temple grounds which are one and one-half streets south of the treasure hall.

Various statues from the temple's earlier buildings give some idea of the riches the temple once enjoyed. Among these images are a seated Amida Nyorai, the gold-leaf covered principal image of the Gango-ji after the 900s, and a six-arm Nyoirin Kannon from the 1200s. Seated on a lotus, the Kannon has one knee raised, one right hand touching its cheek while another hand holds the magic *centamani* jewel and yet another hand holds the Wheel of Life. There are also two images of Prince Shotoku, one at the age of two at his first prayers and one at the age of sixteen, holding a censer as he prays for his dying father, the Emperor Yomei. An X-ray photograph of the two-year-old Shotoku image shows a small *gorinto* (five-tiered stupa) hidden in its right leg. Another image is of Kobo Daishi (Kukai) with a *vajra* (thunderbolt) in one hand and his prayer beads in his other hand, and the image is accompanied by a display of over ninety sheets of religious written materials found within the image.

JURIN-IN

Two streets south of the east side of the Gango-ji and then one-half a street to the east brings one to the small but charming Jurin-in. Once a part of the great Gango-ji monastery, the Jurin-in became independent when the Gango-ji declined after the departure of the capital from Nara in 784. With a pleasant, small garden before it, the Jurin-in is an oasis in a crowded residential area. Within its main hall, an unusual sanctuary of stone slabs with raised, carved religious images upon them adds to the delight of a visit to this intimate temple.

The temple grounds are entered through its Kamakura era (1185–1333) south gate, and the garden with its stone walks and graveled areas with large rocks and well-trimmed bushes about a pond are a pleasant setting for the temple buildings.

HONDO

The Hondo (main hall) is in a building style of the thirteenth century, and it is said to have once been a portion of the imperial palace. It is reputed to have been given to the temple sometime after the founding of the Jurin-in by Asano Nakai in 715, but the building shows the styling of the later Kamakura period. Its attractive, compact size makes it appear to be a residential structure rather than a temple building. The Hondo is entered from its west side, and the jewel of the building is the stone shrine at the rear of the main hall.

The main room of the Hondo acts as a worship hall before the stone chamber of the thirteenth century which is behind this main room. The stone panels of the chamber are carved with images of Shaka and Miroku and Jizo (in mid-interior) as well as bodhisattvas. Over the wide opening of the doorway to the stone unit are inscriptions in circles—the stars with their names. To the side of the structure at the right rear is the figure of Kobo Daishi, to the rear is the Shaka Nyorai, and on the left side is an image of Shobo Ryogen Taishi (founder of the Shugendo sect of Yamabushi [mountain priests] who practice austerities in the mountains).

Outside, to the left of the south gate, is the Fudo-do with a fearsome looking Fudo in a cabinet, rope and sword in hand, accompanied by his two young assistants (*doji*). The hall itself is made impressive through the silver and black brocaded hangings of the altar area.

Behind the Hondo to the right is a small memorial shrine which houses an image of Kobo Daishi. To the right of this is an earthen tumulus with a small opening on its north side into which one can peer at the small Jizo figure carved in stone at the rear interior of the tumulus. If one can believe legends, the child buried here was the offspring of an early Japanese official who had been sent to China—where he became the father of the child. Left behind with his mother when the father returned to Japan, the child is said to have followed his father by crossing the sea from China to Japan on the back of a fish. If that weren't remarkable enough, it is also claimed that the child, whose calligraphy was said to be outstanding, taught the learned ninth-century Kobo Daishi how to write.

BYAKUGO-JI

One last temple of interest in southeast Nara is the Byakugo-ji which is most easily reached by taxi, although bus 122 from the JR station can bring one to the Byakugo-ji bus stop. A small temple overlooking the city, the Byakugo-ji is primarily of interest for the images in its treasure hall.

Founded in 715 by the priest Sonso, the teacher of Kobo Daishi, the location had been the site of the country villa of Prince Shiki-no-Miko, a son of the Emperor Tenchi of the mid-600s. It was transformed into a temple by imperial order after the prince's death, and it was named the Takamadoyama temple after the mountain behind it. It had an Amida Nyorai as its main image as well as a noted Monju figure in its pagoda. During the 1200s, a number of other images were added to the temple, including the noted Emma-o, King of Hell, and his assistants, all of which remain in the treasure hall.

HONDO

The temple grounds are entered by means of a long, uphill, stepped path. At the top of the steps, the Kuri (priests' quarters) is on the right while the Hondo is on the left. A small Jizo hall and the treasure hall are behind the Hondo. The Hondo has a raised platform in its center on which are two Amida and the charming image of Seishi with hands clasped in prayer while a Kannon is in the act of lifting a lotus flower on which to receive the soul of a newly deceased person. Both have their hair piled high in a stylized manner. Images of Fudo and the two-year-old Prince Shotoku saying his first Buddhist prayers are to the left of the main platform.

TREASURE HALL

The modern treasure hall is the most important element of the temple for visitors since the Byakugo-ji's major images are preserved here. Altar tables before the images indicate that this is no mere museum but is a hall of worship as well as a protective center for these ancient religious works of art. In the middle of the hall is the 4.5-foot seated Amida Nyorai with its hands in the mudra of concentration. Formerly the main image of the temple, it has an elaborate aureole behind it on which small Buddha images stand out against the scrolls of the carved background.

On the left side of the hall is the Emma grouping which once stood in a now missing Emma hall. In Amida Buddhism, all beings are reborn after death in one of the Six Realms, the lowest of which is Hell. Hell is presided over by the Ten Kings, each accompanied by his assistants Shimei and Shiroku before whom the sinner is dragged by demons. Emma-o, one of the Ten Kings, is here a seated image of 3.9 feet from the 1200s. This colored, wooden image wears a large bag-like hat with a rod through it, and he holds a staff in his right hand. With richly colored crystal eyes in a large head, his mouth is open and his jaw touches his breast as he scowls in anger at the wrongdoer before him. On the left side of Emma-o, seated on a vermilion stool covered with a lion's skin, is Shiroku reading from an open scroll of the wrongdoings of the being before him. The scroll which was once stretched between his hands is now missing. His associate Shimei also sits on a lion-skin-covered stool holding a long board in his right hand while in his left hand he holds a brush to jot down the sentence being passed on the condemned before him. His ferocious look bodes ill for the miserable victim. An additional one of the Ten Kings, Taizan-o, is nearby.

Further images on the right side of the hall include the seated Monju, 3.3 feet tall, which was once the principal image of the temple's Taho-to pagoda. It is particularly noted for the carved delicacy of the folds of its garments. It once had a jeweled crown (now lost) at the base of its piled-up hair.

Along the western edge of the temple grounds, where the land falls off to the valley below, are tables and seats where one can look over the city and valley—and perhaps enjoy a picnic lunch.

Bus 122 can take one back to the city center.

TOUR

7

Saidai-ji

Akishino-dera

Joruri-ji

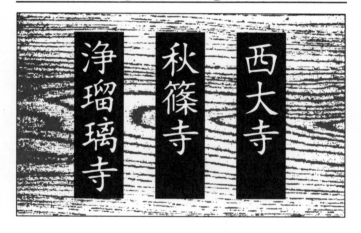

TWO TEMPLES at the western side of Nara and a museum just beyond them, together with a temple to the north of the city limits, and a folk museum to the south of town, compose a varied tour. No doubt it would be well to take the morning bus to the Joruri-ji, the temple to the north of the city, and then to visit the folk museum in the afternoon at Koriyama as a one-day tour. Of the western Nara temples, on another day, the Akishino-dera is noted for its sweet Gigei-ten image while the Saidai-ji, even with much of its glory gone, is of interest because of its connection with an empress who could not resist a handsome priest—and thereby almost lost her throne for a second time. The Yamato Bunkakan is a fine art museum which has a most excellent Asian art collection—the gift to the public by a former president of the Kintetsu Railway.

Alternatively, one could visit the western city sites in conjunction with a visit to the Sogo Department Store on the westward extension of Noborioji. To recommend a visit to a modern department store may seem somewhat out of place in a volume devoted to the historic sites of Nara, but the Sogo Department Store in Nara is in itself historic in that it shows the slick commercial side of a portion of modern Japanese life of the late twentieth century, an aspect which one should experience. Japan may not have had gilded marble halls in its historic past as some European countries did, but it certainly does have them today in its modern shopping centers. The Sogo store is a seven-story building which has everything from a marble-clad first floor to a top floor devoted to various types of restaurants with a world clock which on the hour has compartments on its face which open to permit small figures in the dress of various nations to dance to that modern international hymn of "It's a Small World."

The first floor of the store not only offers the riches of name designers of Europe and the United States (at the usual inflated Japanese price for imports), but it has a golden replica of the Yumedono of the Horyu-ji temple to set the proper tone for a commercial establishment in what was once the religious and historic center of the nation. Thus it is an experience one can enjoy. In good weather, there is also the roof which, as with all Japanese department stores, can offer everything from a place to leave the children in a playground, to a nursery for plants and garden suppplies, to a Shinto shrine, and, in the case of this establishment, a raised, rotating restaurant which permits one while dining to enjoy all of the valley and hills and the ever-spreading growth of Nara City.

If department stores are not your interest, then the day's tour can start with the Saidai-ji, the Great Western Temple.

SAIDAI-JI

When one considers Buddhist temples, one normally thinks of pious donors or sponsors who set in motion the development of a religious complex to enhance the teachings of the Buddha or to honor him in one of his various manifestations. This is not so, however, when it comes to the Saidai-ji which lies just one street to the south of the Yamato Saidai-ji railroad station, for other motives were at work when it was commissioned by the Empress Koken/Shotoku.

The empress was the daughter of the pious Emperor Shomu and Empress Komyo, and she ascended the throne upon her father's abdication in 749. Along with her parents, she was ordained by the priest Ganjin when he set up his ordination platform at the Todai-ji in 754. Reigning during her first period on the throne under the name of the Empress Koken (since she was to abdicate and then return to the throne), she lacked the wisdom and the sense of judgment of Fujiwara-no-Fuhito who was her grandfather on her mother's side and her great-grandfather on her father's side, Shomu's mother being the daughter of Fuhito (by Fuhito's first marriage) and Shomu's wife Komyo also being Fuhito's daughter (by his second marriage). Coming under the influence of Fujiwara-no-Toyonari and his brother Nakamaro, the grandsons of Fuhito, as her leading ministers, the empress was manipulated by Nakamaro as she was to be manipulated by the other leading figure in her life, the priest Dokyo.

Nakamaro convinced Koken that she should abdicate and become a nun, a step she took in 758 when she had her head shaved and entered a nunnery, leaving Nakamaro to manipulate the young Emperor Junnin. Becoming ill, she was attended in 761 by a handsome priest, Dokyo, who seems to have been a faith healer of sorts. She fell in love with Dokyo, and he convinced her (for his own personal reasons and to his benefit) that she should take back the throne. In the ensuing machinations between Nakamaro and Dokyo, Nakamaro planned a coup d'état, was found out, and was killed in an ensuing rebellion in 764. The reigning Emperor Junnin was quickly sent into exile, where he soon died an unnatural death, and the empress re-ascended the throne as the Empress Shotoku.

Dokyo now ruled the land through the empress as he ruled her bed. The nobles as well as the monks at the Todai-ji were displeased with the situation, but the empress continued to shower favors on Dokyo, even to the extent of naming him Ho-o, a title reserved previously only for emperors who had become monks. At Dokyo's urgings, to spite his clerical opponents, the empress decreed the construction of the Saidai-ji, the Great West Temple in west Nara as opposed to the Todai-ji, the Great East Temple in east Nara.

Dokyo's ambitions knew no bounds, and he evidently aspired to the emperorship itself. The empress thought it wise to consult the god Hachiman at Usa in Kyushu before abdicating in Dokyo's favor, sending the trusted Wake-no-Kiyomaro to inquire of Hachiman whether a commoner could become emperor. Dokyo tried to bribe Kiyomaro to return with a favorable oracle, threatening him as well if the answer were in the negative. Kiyomari returned with a pronouncement that the emperorship had to remain with the descendents of the Sun Goddess Amaterasu—and in revenge Dokyo had Kiyomaro's Achilles' tendons cut before having him sent into exile. Shotoku kept the throne, but within a year she was unexpectedly dead, and the nobles had Dokyo exiled. He died in exile within three years. No woman would succeed to the throne for another nine hundred years therafter.

The Saidai-ji was dedicated to the Four Deva Kings (Shitenno) who, the empress felt, had protected the state when Nakamaro had rebelled. No money was spared on construction, though ineptness seemed to be the order of the day. The Shitenno had to be cast a number of times before a perfect set resulted. There were to be two golden halls as large as the Todai-ji Daibutsuden and two pagodas taller than those at the Todai-ji. By 770, once the empress was dead and Dokyo had been banished, these plans had evaporated. The temple languished in its incomplete form, and then a series of fires destroyed the temple structures over time. Though there were successive rebuildings of parts of the complex, the goal of Dokyo and the empress to create a temple to rival and surpass the Todai-ji was never fully realized.

SHIO-DO

One enters the Saidai-ji today through the To-mon, the small East Gate, when coming from the railway station. The first major building on the right is the Shio-do, the hall of the Shitenno. Even the poorly executed Shitenno of the empress' day disappeared in temple fires in time, and today only the demons under the feet of the later replacement images of the Deva Kings are from the original casting. Now the Shitenno, instead of being the primary images of the Shio-do, guard a Senju Kannon (Eleven-Headed Kannon), accompanied by a Fudo image, the Kannon having been moved here from the destroyed Kannon-do.

KONDO

The original two Kondo dedicated to Yakushi and Miroku disappeared in the 900s in a fire, as did the successor to the single Kondo which was rebuilt. Today's Kondo is a 1752 reconstruction with a Shaka Nyorai as its primary image. The building lies well into the grounds and is opposite the base of the former East Pagoda. The Shaka Nyorai is a copy of the image in the Seiryo-ji of Kyoto, the image which is reputed to have threatened to return to China over its displeasure with the civil unrest in Japan in the early 1200s. It is noted for its richly draped robe with folds like running water and the lacy carved aureole behind it.

The Kondo also contains a golden Monju as a child seated on a lotus blossom atop a lion and surrounded by four protectors: a Yuima to the left rear, a Jizo to the right rear, a Zenzai-doji child-assistant to the right front, and an image of Shubodai to the left front. In addition there is a golden Miroku to the far right behind the Shaka, the one-time main image of the second of the two original Kondo. A multi-arm Fudo is at the rear of the hall as well.

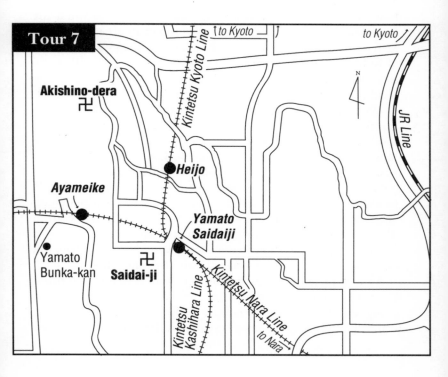

PAGODA BASE

The base of the East Pagoda is still intact, and it is of interest since, although the base is square, the outline of the intended octagonal base surrounds the present square base. Planned as an octagonal pagoda with a diameter of 88.6 feet, to rise seven stories and thus exceed the more than 300 foot height of the Todai-ji pagodas, and to be topped with a blue tile roof, the plans never worked out. Instead, two five-story conventional small pagodas were built, legend claiming that its architect was condemned to hell because of the change of plans. Neither pagoda lasted too long before being consumed by fire.

AIZEN-DO

The Aizen-do is a structure to the west of and facing the pagoda base, a unit which was moved to Nara from Kyoto when the Kamakura government ordered all temples to create an Aizen Myo-o image as a plea for the subjugation of the invading forces of Kublai Khan which threatened to invade Japan. In 1274 and again in 1281 impressive services were held at the Saidai-ji to help ward off the Mongol invasion of Kyushu.

According to a temple tradition, on the last day of services to Aizen Myo-o, on July 4, 1281, an arrow held by the image suddenly flew to the west, thereby causing the defeat of the Mongol invaders. Other more historical accounts credited the *kamikaze*, the divine wind or typhoon which sank the Mongol boats as being more responsible for the defeat of the invaders. A view of this fearful red-colored Aizen Myo-o would no doubt have been enough to stop any invasion: two teeth protrude from Aizen's upper jaw, his hair stands on end and is crowned with a dragon's head on top. For centuries it was a hidden image, but today it may be seen on January 11 and February 4.

A more pleasant image in this same hall is that of the priest Eison who rebuilt the temple in the 1200s and oriented it to Shingon Buddhism with its Fudo and Myo-o images. This lifelike, seated, painted wooden image created in 1280 shows Eison at age

79 with a fly whisk, the symbol of priestly authority, in his hand. Eison completely rebuilt the temple, and when he died at ninety, his ashes were placed beneath a small stupa in the northwest corner of the temple grounds. His rebuilt temple was, of course, consumed in flames in the years after his death, the 1502 fire being particularly devastating.

SHUHO-KAN

The Shuho-kan, the temple treasure house, is open at the end of October and early November at the same time the Shoso-in treasures in Nara are on view. It has a few interesting objects among which are the four small Buddhas which once sat within the base of the East Pagoda, a seated image of the priest Gyogi, and a standing Kichijo-ten image. In addition there are pictures, other small sculptures, and various religious objects from former structures of this temple.

Aside from the January 11 and February 4 viewing of the Aizen Myo-o and the autumn opening of the treasure house, the Ochamori Ceremony on the second Saturday and Sunday in April and in November is famous. A special tea ceremony is held in which tea is made in a gigantic tea bowl, the tea having been whipped with a huge tea whisk. This humorous tea ceremony is very popular and draws huge crowds.

AKISHINO-DERA

The Akishino-dera is a small temple in the northern part of the town of Yamato Saidai-ji. It is easiest to reach it by taking a taxi, and one can then walk back to the rail station or take the bus which stops in front of the temple. Why visit the Akishino-dera? For four reasons: it is the last temple which was built in Nara before the capital was moved to Nagaoka and then to Kyoto; its Hondo is one of the two remaining original temple buildings of the period between 710 and 784 in Nara; it holds the lovely Gigei-ten figure; and it is the home of the fearful Daigensui Myo-o.

HONDO

This main hall is a thirteenth-century rebuilding of the temple's original Kodo (lecture hall), all that remained after an 1182 fire. Its eleven Buddhist images are arranged in a row at the back of the hall. The Yakushi, the Buddha of Medicine and Healing, being its main image, has the ample proportions which show the influence of Tang Chinese artistic style. Seated on a pedestal, it has its right hand raised granting absence of fear while its left hand holds the traditional medicine pot. On either side of the Yakushi are Bon-ten and Taishaku-ten with dry-lacquer heads of the 700s but wooden bodies of the 1200s. Next, on either side of these images are stands each with six of the Twelve Divine Generals.

Further to the left is a Jizo and then the noted Gigei-ten whose dry-lacquer head was created at the end of the 700s but whose wooden body is of thirteenth-century derivation. Standing seven feet tall, she is one of the more attractive images of the end of the Nara era, and her appealing quality comes from her lovely face and the slight inclination of her head. To the right end of the images, beyond the generals, is a Fudo Myo-o and then a Kichijo-ten. At the right rear is a lacquered cabinet containing a many-arm Myo-o, the gilded interior of the cabinet showing lotus leaves rising from the water. On the far left is an additional Myo-o with two fierce companions guarding him. The number of Myo-o images indicates the influence of Shingon Buddhism of the post-800 era on this temple.

DAIGENSUI MYO-O-DO

To the left of the ticket booth as one enters the temple inner grounds is the small Daigensui Myo-o-do which contains the 6.5-foot-tall single faced, six-armed Myo-o clad only in a waist cloth. His face shows the fury he feels against evil, his hair stands on end, and the snakes twined about his neck and legs are meant to scare away the evil which might be able to withstand his fierce face. This is the oldest Myo-o image in Japan, and it is only on view from May 1 to May 15. Related to it, to the east of the Hondo is the Kozuikaku or Holy Water Pavilion. It shelters the Akai well in which Priest Jogyo saw the Daigensui Myo-o on the surface of the water in the mid-800s when he was reciting the Daigensui Myo-o prayer—the image which is copied in the building at the other end of the temple grounds.

YAMATO BUNKA-KAN

The Yamato Bunka-kan is a museum of Asian art which opened in 1960 in a most pleasant modern building created in the external style of a traditional *kura* (storage building). It is just a short walk from Ayameike Station. With more than twenty thousand objects of sculpture, ceramics, lacquer, paintings, prints, textiles, and calligraphy, the museum offers changing exhibitions seven times a year from its own collections as well as from other noted collections. Its exhibitions are always first rate, and these should not be missed by anyone interested in Asian art.

NARA PREFECTURAL MUSEUM OF FOLK CULTURE

In 1974 Nara Prefecture created a Museum of Folk Culture similar to the open-air villages which other countries have developed. This museum outside of Koriyama City, just a few miles south of Nara, deals with life in Nara Prefecture before the industrial revolution of the late nineteenth century affected Nara. The modern museum building with its fine displays of traditional crafts and manner of work is complemented by a series of farm and town buildings in its outdoor museum on the extensive grounds. This is a delightful complex which is quite different from the many shrines and temples for which Nara is noted. It is an outdoor museum which should not be missed.

The museum is most easily reached by taking either the JR train to Koriyama or the Kintetsu Line train from Yamato Saidai-ji to Koriyama. (The two stations are at different locations in Koriyama.) From the station a taxi can be taken to the museum which is to the west of Koriyama City. After visiting the museum, a bus from the main road before the museum grounds can be taken back to the town and the station.

JORURI-JI

The Joruri-ji is a forty-five minute bus ride from Nara. Bus 111 starts from the JR station in Nara, but the bus does not always have its number marked on it, and it is best to obtain a schedule of its departure and return times from the tourist office on Sanjo-dori—and to obtain in writing the Japanese characters which mark the destination of the bus if the bus does not bear the number 111. The return is simpler since the Joruri-ji is the terminal for the route.

As can be discerned from the number of Yakushi images and the various temples which hold this image as their central deity, Yakushi, the Buddha of Medicine and Healing, was one of the more important of the Buddhist deities in the 600s and 700s. So it was with the Joruri-ji also, its main image on its founding in the 700s being a Yakushi. In time, with the spread of Buddhism among the people, a less theologically oriented religion with simpler doctrines was bound to evolve, and thus the reverence of Amida came into popularity. Salvation did not need learning under faith in Amida, nor did it involve religious practices. One merely had to believe in Amida, and perhaps say the *Nembutsu* prayer after Honen evolved this doctrine—and one would be welcomed after death into Amida's Western Paradise.

Although the Joruri-ji was established in 743 by Gyogi, the priest who received the vision from Amaterasu at Ise which permitted the construction of the Todai-ji temple, its main hall is recorded as a 1047 structure with a small wooden Yakushi at its center. That image today is in the base of the temple pagoda. The present eleven-bay hall was created in 1107 when, under the growing interest in the Buddha Amida, the main emphasis of the temple changed and the image of Amida became all important. A number of temples were built in the 800s through the 1200s which had nine Amida images in a row in their Hondo, but of these the Joruri-ji alone remains, its nine Amida figures still in place. These nine images represent the nine stages of nirvana through which souls can pass. In the early days, worshippers could not enter the Hondo but had to pray from across the pond which stands before the Hondo as they faced to the west, the pond symbolizing the separation of this world from the world of Amida's Western Paradise.

HONDO

Today the Hondo, the temple's main hall, can be entered, and it is a very simple structure, thereby making the nine gilded Amidas the focus of attention. The central Amida is eight feet tall and thus is larger than the four Amida on either side who are 7.3 feet in size. The central Amida holds his hands in the *raigo-in* mudra, welcoming the souls of the dead to his Western Paradise. The other eight Amida hold their hands in the mudra of contemplation. In the left-hand corner of the hall are two images of the Shitenno guardians while a Fudo Myo-o and his Doji attendant are on the right. This Fudo was once the main figure in the now lost Goma-do hall. A Jizo image and a Kichijo-ten complete the images on the platform, the Kichijo-ten only being placed on view from January 1 to 15, from March 21 to May 20, and from November 1 to November 30.

POND AND PAGODA

The Hondo lies on the western side of the pond which has an island in its midst with a small Shinto shrine upon it to offer the protection of the local kami to the temple. On either side of the pond is a stone lantern from the 1300s dedicated to the deities of the Hondo and the pagoda. On the far side of the pond is the three-story pagoda which is 53 feet tall, and it contains the temple's earlier main image of Yakushi, Lord of the Joruri or Eastern Paradise. The Yakushi image is on view on the eighth day of each month if the weather permits. The pagoda was originally erected in Kyoto in the 1100s but it was brought here in that same century to hold the Yakushi image as the orientation of the temple changed to the worship of Amida.

If one is energetic, one can walk the two-thirds of a mile to the Gansen-ji along a path lined with ancient Buddhist images—so long as one keeps in mind the return bus schedule for the trip back to Nara.

Horyu-ji · Chugu-ji
Horin-ji

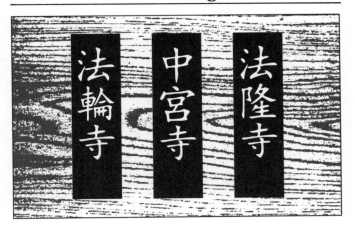

E VERY NATION has an individual who has helped to shape the character of his people and the institutions of his time as well as set patterns for generations yet to come. Japan is no exception. Prince Shotoku (572–622) was the far-seeing leader who is remembered not only for his achievements in establishing Buddhism within the land, but for his concern for Confucian ethics and Confucian statesmanship which was eventually to lead to the creation of the Japanese nation-state.

As a youth of sixteen, he was involved in the battle which made possible the establishment of Buddhism in Japan despite the opposition of those clan leaders who, secure in the traditional native religion, feared this new religion which had come from Korea and China. Named the regent for his aunt, the Empress Suiko, in 593 when he was twenty-one, he fixed the court ranks to bring order to the clan society of his day, and he is said to have promulgated the Confucian Constitution of Seventeen Articles which set the course of Japanese government in the direction of an organized state. He sent an embassy to China so that Japan could learn from the advanced culture of that continental power, and he himself became proficient in Chinese so as to help to further learning in Japan.

HORYU-JI

In 601 the prince built a palace at Ikaruga, some eight miles south of present-day Nara, and six years later in 607, adjacent to this mansion, he created the Wakakusa-dera temple. This temple was one of the earliest of Buddhist temples in Japan, and it ranked with the Hoko-ji temple built in 588 in Asuka, twelve miles to the south, and the Shitenno-ji of 592 in Naniwa (Osaka) with whose creation he was also involved. The Wakakusa-dera, the predecessor to the Horyu-ji temple, burned to the ground in 670, long after Shotoku's death, and its successor is the present Horyu-ji. The name of the temple, Horyu-ji (Temple of the Way of Learning), indicates its purpose: that of serving as an educational center where lectures on Buddhism would be given and from which the new religion would spread throughout the land.

The Horyu-ji was built by workmen from Paekche, Korea, craftsmen experienced in the finest temple construction, and the buildings of the Horyu-ji were aligned in continental fashion with the North Star since temples were meant to be arranged in a north-south direction. The temple pagoda and Kondo (golden or main hall) from the post-670 rebuilding (after the fire which destroyed the earlier temple) are the oldest wooden buildings in existence, and they are among the most important architectural treasures in Japan. Additional structures were added in later centuries, and today forty buildings exist at the Horyu-ji, and the collection of early Buddhist sculpture and art it has amassed through the centuries ranks among the most important in Japan.

Bus 52 or 60 from the bus terminal on Noborioji behind the Kintetsu Nara Station take one to the Horyu-ji in about thirty minutes. The bus stop at the Horyu-ji is announced in English on the bus, and the path to the Horyu-ji from the bus leads along a fairly recent esplanade with souvenir shops and restaurants to the entrance to the temple. The Horyu-ji complex is divided into two sections, the Sai-in (West Precinct) and the To-in (East Precinct), and of the present forty buildings, the oldest are the pagoda and the Kondo, which date from the post-670 era. The fireproof treasure hall, on the other hand, was built in 1949. The older buildings have undergone restoration during the second half of the twentieth century, and the pagoda and the Kondo, for example, have been totally dismantled and repaired in the course of their restoration.

NANDAI-MON AND CHU-MON

The Nandai-mon, the Great South Gate, leads from the esplanade before the temple entry into a long path between walls to the main east-west walkway within the temple grounds. Various temple buildings lie behind these walls, and the foundations of the 607 Wakakusa-dera have been unearthed in the private area beyond the wall on the right-hand side of the path, that original temple having been destroyed in the fire of 670. Its floor plan followed the so-called Shitenno-ji pattern of Naniwa (Osaka) and Korea with the pagoda in the center of the complex with a Yakushi image in its Kondo, a plan not followed when the Horyu-ji replaced the Wakakusa-dera after the 670 fire.

Crossing the east-west path which runs through the temple grounds, the route from the Nandai-mon continues to the Chu-mon, the Central Gate, in the center of the Kairo (roofed corridors) which surround the central and most important portion of the Horyu-ji. The Chu-mon is a four-bay gateway whose columns show the entasis (swelling at the center) which is a characteristic of early Buddhist architecture in Japan—some say it is a Greek influence which crossed the Silk Road to the East. The two middle sections of the gate permit a view of the pagoda and the Kondo. The end bays each contain ferocious-looking Nio

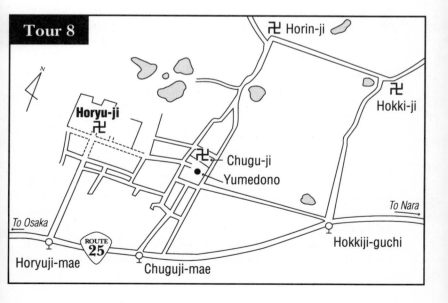

(Guardian Kings) with scowling faces and rippling muscles, standing guard against the forces of evil which might impinge upon the sacred grounds beyond the Chu-mon. Completed in 711, these are the oldest free-standing Nio images in Japan. To their left, at the west end of the Kairo, is the entry to the temple's main courtyard where the ticket counter is situated.

PAGODA

The entry corridor leading to the Chu-mon brings one to the inner courtyard of the Horyu-ji. Ahead, the pagoda lies on the left and the Kondo is on the right while the Kodo (lecture hall) is straight ahead to the north beyond these two buildings. The Kairo (corridors) encircle the courtyard on the south, east, and west while the Kodo completes the northern side of the central courtyard.

A pagoda is an architectural form which began in India as a squat stupa built over a relic of the remains of the historic Buddha. In China it developed into a high-rise memorial tower, and it was this latter form which the Japanese were to employ. When the Horyu-ji pagoda was dismantled for repairs in 1949, a small relic chamber 9.8 feet beneath the pagoda was uncovered. Within, the relics had been placed in a small glass bottle (which was empty), and this was enclosed first in an egg-shaped gold and silver container, and then in a globular bronze unit. In addition to the religious items, a *repoussé* plaque, a copper bowl, a gold plaque, and 272 beads and 627 pearls were found.

The pagoda stands five-stories tall at 107 feet above its relic chamber, and its wide, overhanging roofs are tapered upwards so that its fifth (top) roof is almost one-half the size of the roof over the first floor. This tapering of the roof sizes gives the impression that the pagoda is even taller than it is. Space was left between the four corner posts of the pagoda base so as to create four grotto-like areas with scenes illustrating events associated with the historic Buddha (Gautama—or Sakyamuni, his Indian clan name). In the east bay there is a religious discussion between the

Bodhisattva Monju and Yuima, a layman learned in Buddhist law, with onlookers on their knees listening to the debate. The north bay depicts the death of the Buddha. The gilded Buddha image is here shown stretched on a low bed-like platform, and an old woman kneels in front of his body while his grieving disciples bemoan his death. The west bay shows the distribution of the relics of the Buddha, his disciples kneeling on either side of a coffer and reliquary. The south and last bay shows the Paradise of the Buddha Miroku, the Buddha of the Future. In addition to these small figures, the interior of the pagoda was at one time covered with wall paintings, but these have faded with the centuries.

KONDO

The Kondo of the Horyu-ji is the most important building of the monastery not only because it is the oldest wooden building in Japan but for its architectural attractiveness and the art treasures it contains. This double-roofed building is the best surviving example of Asuka period (552–645) architectural style. A two-level structure, its columns have a noticeable swelling in the center (entasis) as is true of the Chu-mon columns also. The eaves of the second roof project fourteen feet from the post centers, and thus during the Edo period (1603–1868) external supports were added to brace the roof which had begun to sag. Twisting dragon carvings were placed around these supports as a decorative element.

The Kondo is divided into three sections: the center unit holds the Shaka triad, the eastern part has a Yakushi Nyorai image, while the western portion has a later Amida image of the 1200s. Three great canopies hang over the images, each double-roofed and enlivened with figures of heavenly musicians. The Shaka triad of the seated Buddha Sakyamuni (Shaka) with a bodhisattva on either side is the crowning work of Shiba Tori, the earliest sculptor in bronze in Japan. An inscription on the back of the Shaka indicates that it was made in 623 at the orders of the

Empress Suiko to pray for the peaceful repose of Prince Shotoku's soul. It had originally been commissioned by the empress as a votive offering for the recovery of the prince from illness, but after his death in 622 it was cast by the ciré perdue (lost wax) method and given as an offering for his rebirth in paradise.

The Shaka image is noted for its archaic smile and its frozen draperies. Its head has the customary marks of the Buddha: the top cranial protuberance delineating supernatural wisdom, the third eye of foreknowledge, and the long ear lobes stretched by the heavy gold earrings as were worn by the nobility of India. Its right hand is raised in the mudra which banishes fear or grants reassurance, while its left hand is in the mudra of granting wishes.

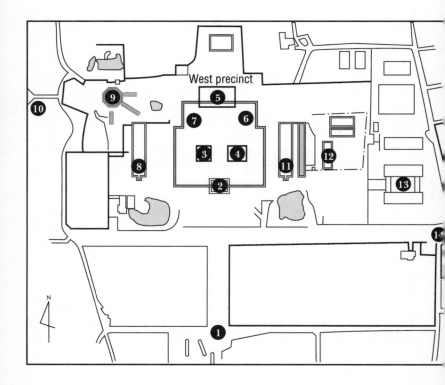

The stylized robes of the Shaka lap over his body and the front of the pedestal. The attendant bodhisattvas each stands on a lotus blossom, and each holds a magic jewel, the *centamani,* in their left hands, while the crowns on their heads are reminiscent of the crowns of the Sasanian kings of Persia. A huge aureole in the shape of a cobra's hood rises behind all three images, the central design on it behind the Shaka is in the form of a lotus which serves as a halo. Seven small, seated Buddhas are worked into the design of the aureole which is further enriched with abstract designs and patterns of curved lines.

To the right of the triad is the Yakushi image which was the main image in the original Wakakusa-dera of 607. An inscription

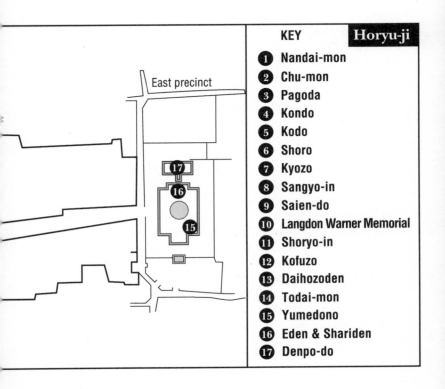

KEY   **Horyu-ji**

1. Nandai-mon
2. Chu-mon
3. Pagoda
4. Kondo
5. Kodo
6. Shoro
7. Kyozo
8. Sangyo-in
9. Saien-do
10. Langdon Warner Memorial
11. Shoryo-in
12. Kofuzo
13. Daihozoden
14. Todai-mon
15. Yumedono
16. Eden & Shariden
17. Denpo-do

East precinct

on its aureole states "Made by Prince Shotoku and Empress Suiko for the Emperor Yomei," and it is dated 607. Yomei was Shotoku's father, and in his last illness he requested Shotoku and Suiko (his sister) to build a temple as a votive offering for his recovery. He died shortly thereafter (in 593), and the Horyu-ji in a sense is the temple which he requested but which was not built until fourteen years after his death. The Yakushi image is a dignified, seated figure with the same broad nose and frozen drapery as is seen on the Shaka image. It too would be the work of Shiba Tori.

To the left of the triad is an Amida image by Kosho of the 1200s, Amidaism gradually replacing Yakushi as a central figure in Japanese Buddhism at this time (see the Joruri-ji for a discussion of this change). In each corner of the image platform stands one of the four Shitenno (Guardian Kings), the oldest such images in Japan. Carved from one block of camphor wood, the images are stiff in stance, and each stands on the back of a crouching demon. Their expressionless faces and the crude carving of the figures are offset by their richly decorated surfaces and the open metalwork of their helmets.

The Horyu-ji was always noted for its early frescoes, but any wooden building is susceptible to decay and needs to be restored. Thus in 1934 the decision was made to dismantle the Kondo and to restore it. Because of the Second World War, the task took twenty years to complete. As a part of the preservation efforts, it was agreed that the famed frescoes on the Kondo walls would be documented in case they should ever be damaged or destroyed. The work of restoring the Kondo was first started in 1944 and then not re-initiated until 1947. Early on the morning of January 26, 1949, a short circuit in an electrically heated cushion, used by the artist to warm himself while copying the frescoes, started a fire. Firemen were able to save the Kondo, but the heat and the flames burned away the delicate color pigments of the frescoes or bleached them so badly that these 1,200-year-old treasures were ruined. Fortunately, the statuary had previously been removed.

In 1966 the *Asahi Shimbun* newspaper received permission to have reproductions of the frescoes made for the Kondo, and these reproductions were installed in 1968. The influences of China, of Central Asia, and of India have all been traced as the sources of the artistic style of these frescoes. Each wall depicts one of the four paradises of the Buddha world: Shaka (east wall), Amida (west wall), Yakushi (northwest wall), and Miroku (northeast wall), and these were supplemented by eight smaller panels of standing bodhisattvas on other wall spaces.

KODO

The Lecture Hall was an essential part of any monastery, for here the monks of the four sects of early Japanese Buddhism gathered for study and lectures on the sacred texts of the faith. The present Kodo was brought from Kyoto in 990, and it is the largest building in the Horyu-ji. Within are the images of the 8.5-foot-tall Yakushi Nyorai and the Bodhisattvas Nikko and Gakko of the same height. There is also an image of Kanroka, a priest from Korea who was a friend and mentor of Prince Shotoku. Two Chinese-style, stepped and roofed lecterns stand before the image dais, platforms from which the abbot can discuss theological points with the monks of the temple.

KYOZO AND SHORO

Two other small units make up a part of the inner courtyard of the central portion of the West Precinct. To the left, when facing the Kodo, is the Shoro or bell tower, now an integral part of the corridor although it was once free-standing. It holds one of the oldest bronze bells in Japan (707–728). To the right is the Kyozo, the sutra-storage building, which holds copies of the Tripitaka scriptures of Buddhism.

Behind the Kodo is the Kami-no-mido, a hall from the 1200s which holds a wooden Shaka image and two bodhisattvas, all three guarded by the four Shitenno.

SANGYO-IN

A long, low building running parallel to the western side of the west corridor of the central precinct is a rebuilding from the 1200s of the original dormitory structure. The rear portion serves as the monks' dormitory while the front portion is the Sangyo-in, the Tripitaka Hall. Within is a wooden, gold-leaf-covered image of Prince Shotoku lecturing on the sutras. There is a seated, golden Amida Nyorai of the 1100s and a seated Miroku. These images are protected by two colored, wooden guardians. Lectures are given here each year for a period of ninety days beginning on May 16.

SAIEN-DO

To the northwest of the Sangyo-in, on a hillside reached by a stone stairway, is the Saien-do, the West Octagonal Hall, on a granite platform. It is also called the Mine-no-Yakushi, the Healer of the Hill, since the hall has a Yakushi as its main image. Built in 1294 and dedicated to Princess Tachibana, the consort of Prince Shotoku, the seated Yakushi image is an eighth-century hollow, dry-lacquer figure holding a medicine pot in his left hand. The aureole behind him is decorated with the One thousand Buddhas. To the right of Yakushi is a Thousand-Arm Kannon from about 1080, and on the right is a Jizo from before 1080, the oldest Jizo image in Japan. These three images are surrounded and protected by the Twelve Divine Generals dating from the beginning of the twelfth century.

South of the Sangyo-in is a walled area containing monastic buildings not open to the public. Here is the Oyuya, the monastic bathhouse; the Kyakuden, the monastic guest house; and ancillary monastic structures.

LANGDON WARNER MEMORIAL

To the west of the Saien-do, outside the Sai-in walls, is a memorial stone to Langdon Warner, the art historian of Harvard University who has mistakenly been credited by the Japanese with saving

Nara and Kyoto from World War II bombing. (It was U.S. Secretary of War Henry Stimson who was responsible for sparing these cities.)

SHORYO-IN
Returning past the central portion of the Sai-in with the pagoda and Kondo, the Higashi-muro and the Shoryo-in are parallel to the east corridor of the central part of the Sai-in. These two units are part of a long, low, single-story building which is divided into two sections. The rear portion, the Higashi-muro, is a dormitory for monks while the front part is the Shoryo-in worship hall. The Higashi-muro was built at the end of the 600s, reputedly using some of the wood of the original Wakakusa-dera temple. It was rebuilt in 1365, and it retains the actual living quarters of the early monks since four of its eight original cells are intact.

The Shoryo-in, the Hall of the Prince's Soul, is in memory of Prince Shotoku. Within, the rear of the hall is decorated with orange-and-gold hangings upon which the white, sixteen-petal imperial chrysanthemum is worked. To the left of the altar is a hanging scroll of the seated, mature prince while to the right is one of Shotoku as a boy. Within a cabinet is a seated wooden statue of the adult prince, together with a seated Nyoirin Kannon and a standing Jizo. There are also images in the hall of Shotoku's son Yamashiro-no-Miko in priest's robes; of Shotoku's brother Eguri-no-Miko holding a box and armed with a sword; of Mandano-no-Miko holding Shotoku's sword; and of Shotoku's teacher, the Korean priest Egi with a censer in his hand. All the figures are from the 900–1200 era. Shotoku's continuing fame can be attested to by the line of pilgrims waiting at the Shoryo-in desk to have their pilgrim's album stamped. Held regularly each March 23 there is a three-day service here for the repose of Shotoku's soul.

Parallel to the Higashi-muro is the Tsuma-muro on the east, an additional dormitory for monks. To the east of this is a small shrine to Shotoku's horse.

KOFUZO

East of the dormitories is the Kofuzo, the original treasure house for the temple. Built in the traditional *azekura* or log-cabin style, it consists of two units joined under one roof and raised above the ground to permit for air circulation. After the 1949 fire in the Kondo, the government made a concerted effort to help in the creation of fireproof storage buildings for important artistic treasures of the nation. Thus the temple's treasured objects were moved for their safety from the former treasure hall to the new fireproof Daihozoden (Great Treasure Storehouse).

DAIHOZODEN

More than ten thousand items make up the holdings of the Horyu-ji treasure hall, and these are now installed in the fireproof and earthquake-proof Daihozoden which is generally open from 8:00 a.m. to 5:00 p.m. but from 8:00 a.m. to 4:00 p.m. between November 20 and March 10. A pamphlet explaining the items in the hall is available in English at the ticket booth at the entry to the hall. The treasures are too numerous to list, but some of the major items are listed below.

Building 1

- ROOM 1 exhibits artifacts from the original Wakakusa-dera.

- ROOM 2 contains a statue of Prince Shotoku as a child, eighth-century Gigaku masks, a seventh-century bronze sword, and the painting of Shotoku and his two sons. This latter painting is the most reproduced painting from the collection. It shows Shotoku holding a *shaku* (wand of office) while his two young sons have their hair tied in the fashion for youths of the day.

- ROOM 3 contains various images from the Asuka (552–645) era, in particular the Yumetegai Kannon. This latter image is a late 1600s bronze sculpture of the Dream-Changing Kannon which was once the central image in the Eden, the portrait hall of the East Precinct. Those who pray to it can have nightmares changed into pleasant dreams.

- ROOM **4** houses the Kudara Kannon, the most famous work in the treasure hall; its elongated and willowy form is entirely different from the styling of the Shaka triad in the Kondo. It supposedly came from Kudara (Korea), and there is nothing its equal in China or Korea today. A large lotus-blossom halo is behind its head, and it wears a crown of filigree bronze and has a bronze neck piece. It holds a large phial in its left hand.

Building 2

- ROOM **1** contains a drawing of the Horyu-ji after 670; a wall scroll of Prince Shotoku at sixteen; figures of an angel, *apsaras*, and a phoenix from the Kondo; and photographic copies of the Kondo frescoes.

- ROOM **2** exhibits include the Four Deva Kings (Shitenno) from the 700s; a Bon-ten, a Senju Kannon, a Taishaku-ten, and the Tamamushi Shrine.

  The Tamamushi Shrine from the 650s is a model of a type of building which once existed in Japan but has now entirely disappeared; it is a miniature palace or Kondo prior to 670. The paintings on the side of the base are of the Asuka period (552–645) and thus are among the earliest surviving Japanese paintings. The front panels show two monks making offerings from long-handled censers to the relics of the Buddha while flying angels holding an incense burner are overhead. The rear panel shows Mt. Sumeru rising from the sea. A palace is at the foot of the mountain with a dragon on its top and dragons and phoenixes about it. Four hills on the peak hold the palaces of the Four Deva Kings, while atop the mount is the paradise of Taishaku-ten. Clouds, angels, flying horses, phoenixes, holy men riding birds, and the sun and the moon fill out the composition. The side panels are from the *Sutra of the Great*

Nirvana and the *Sutra of the Golden Light.* The most famous panel has the legendary tale portraying the Buddha casting himself off a cliff in compassion in order to feed hungry tiger cubs with his own body. The edges of the panels and other parts of the shrine have bronze filagree strips under which nine thousand emerald-green iridescent wings of the *tamamushi* beetle were once set.

The shrine sits atop the base (as described above) with a heavy, overhanging, tiled, gabled roof. There are double doors on three sides, the doors having bodhisattvas painted upon them, elongated figures holding a lotus stalk. The rear panel has the Buddha preaching the *Lotus Sutra* on Vulture Peak. The inner portion of the shrine is decorated with the One-thousand Buddhas in bronze *repoussé.*

ROOM **3** contains images of an eleventh-century Shaka Nyorai, a Yakushi Nyorai, an Amida Nyorai, and a Sho Kannon (from the 900s), and the Lady Tachibana Shrine.

Lady Tachibana was the wife of Fujiwara-no-Fuhito, the first minister at the time of the creation of the new capital of Heijo-kyo (Nara), and she was the mother of the Empress Komyo, the consort of the Emperor Shomu. Her shrine has a two-layer base, the upper portion of the base being decorated with bodhisattvas and other disciples of the Buddha. Above this double base is a larger rectangular box with double-fold doors. Within the box, the bronze floor is engraved to look like the surface of a pond with its watery surface broken by lotus pads and flowers. On the large center blossom sits Amida with the Bodhisattvas Seishi and Kannon on separate blossoms alongside of him. Behind the three images is a bronze screen on which souls in paradise sit on lotus flowers in great contentment. Of the original eight paneled doors, six remain. The side doors have images of the Shitenno on the outside and four bodhisattvas on the inside. The front panels had Kongo Rikishi (Guardian Kings) on the outside and Buddhas on the inside. The rear doors had angels on the outside and bodhisattvas on the inside.

TO-IN

The path from the Daihozoden leads to the east to the Todaimon (Great East Gate) which provides an entry from the West Precinct (Sai-in) to the East Precinct (To-in) of the Horyu-ji. Prince Shotoku's palace once stood where the East Precinct is now located until it was destroyed by order of Soga-no-Iruka in 643. Almost one hundred years later the East Precinct was built on the palace site as a memorial to Shotoku by Gyoshin for the sake of the prince's soul. He was assisted in this project by the Empress Komyo and her mother the Lady Tachibana, Fujiwara-no-Fuhito's wife. The empress and her mother donated an imperial residence hall of the palace in 739, and this became the Denpo-do, a lecture hall for the East Precinct.

The East Precinct originally had the normal Buddhist temple configuration: a Nandai-mon (south gate), a Chu-mon (middle gate), the Yumedono (dream hall) as its Kondo (golden or main hall), the Denpo-do (lecture hall), and three dormitories. The Yumedono at first was surrounded by its corridors on all four sides, but between 784 and 1334 an Eden (hall of paintings) and the Shari-den (relic hall) replaced the northern portion of the corridor to create the present layout of the East Precinct. During that same period, a Shoro (bell tower) and a Raido (worship hall) were added to the complex as the cult of the worship of Shotoku developed and became popular—and led to prosperity for the temple.

A dragon fountain to provide for purification before entering the Yumedono is at the entrance to the west gate of the Kairo which surrounds the Yumedono. On the left, outside the corridor and its gateway, is the Shoro (bell tower) in the spreading-skirt style with a bell (c. 730) with "Chugu-ji" upon it. One enters the inner precinct through the Sai-mon, the west gate, of the Kairo instead of using the Nan-mon, the south gate, as was originally planned, for the Nan-mon was only used on ceremonial occasions. The Chu-mon or middle gate on the south side has been turned into the Raido, the worship hall where reverence can be made to the Yumedono to its north.

YUMEDONO

The Yumedono is an octagonal building which is on the site of the prince's Ikaruga Palace. According to tradition, it was at this site in his palace that the prince would sit in meditation upon difficult problems of the Buddhist sutras and theology. Here in his dreams would come the answers he sought, and thus the memorial hall to his spirit was named the Yumedono, the Hall of Dreams.

The hall is raised on a double, octagonal stone platform with stone stairways on four sides leading to double doors. The overhanging roof bears a sacred bronze urn with rays emanating from the sacred jewel on its top. From the eaves hang bronze wind bells, the oldest of their kind in existence. Such octagonal buildings with a magic jewel on the top became the model for memorial halls in other temples in time.

Within the Yumedono on the right is a colored, dry-lacquer image of the seated priest Gyoshin who created this building in 739. A second image is of the monk Dosen who was a scholar at the Horyu-ji and who restored the temple in 839. A figure of Shotoku at sixteen is in a case on the east side of the Yumedono. The most important image is that of the standing Guze Kannon which was dedicated by the Empress Komyo in 737. A *hibutsu* or hidden image, it was considered so sacred that not even the temple priests were allowed to see it. Wrapped in 295 feet of white cloth, it remained hidden until 1884 when Ernest Fenellosa, an American art professor in the employment of the Meiji government unwrapped it for the first time. (With its anti-Buddhist bent, the government did not honor temple sensibilities.)

Covered with gold leaf, the Guze Kannon image was intact due to its being a hidden image. Its almond-shaped eyes and broad-nosed face are crowned by a large filigree coronet enhanced with blue glass beads. Its aureole is of gilt bronze open-work, as is its diadem which is decorated with small bells. Its hands are clasped about a *centamani* jewel, and draperies (in wood) are looped over its forearm, reaching to the ground. It is one of the finest works from the Asuka period (552–645), and it is on view from April 11 to May 15 and from October 22 to November 20 annually. It is supposedly a portrait of Prince Shotoku, and one tradition even claims that it was carved by the prince himself.

Beyond the Guze Kannon is a Sho Kannon meant to stand before the Guze Kannon as an attendant.

EDEN AND SHARIDEN

Two buildings take the place of the former north corridor about the Yumedono, and these are the Eden, the portrait hall, and the Shariden, the relic hall. Originally one building, they held the personal possessions of Prince Shotoku.

The Eden has the life story of Shotoku painted on its panelled doors. The ninth/tenth century originals were given to the Imperial Household Agency, and the present paintings are Edo period (1603–1868) copies of a 1219 copy. The building is divided into an outer and an inner shrine. The separate Shariden holds relics of the prince. These two buildings are generally not open to the public.

DENPO-DO

The Denpo-do is the Hall of the Buddha's Teachings, and it was originally a royal residence, that of Lady Tachibana, the Empress Komyo's mother and the wife of Fujiwara-no-Fuhito. Given to the temple in 739 by Komyo and her mother, it serves as the temple's lecture hall. It has three Amida triads on a long altar platform, and, in all, there are twenty statues including a Yakushi, a Shaka, and a Miroku.

CHUGU-JI

Tradition claims that the Chugu-ji nunnery was built on the site of the residence of Prince Shotoku's mother, the Empress Anahobe-no-Hashihito no Himemiko, the consort of the Emperor Yomei. It is said that on her death in 621, just a few months before the prince himself died, he had her palace converted into a nunnery for the repose of her soul. The original palace which became a nunnery, however, was to the east of the present site of the Chugu-ji. The nunnery was moved here and restored by the nun Shinnyo in the 1200s. Traditionally, a member of the imperial family served as the chief nun of the Chugu-ji until 1868 when the *monzeki* tradition was abolished.

The nunnery grounds are entered from the Yumedono area into a tiny but lovely garden of gravel and pines behind pounded-earth walls. Old buildings of the nunnery are about the garden. The path from the entry gate leads to the modern, moated treasure hall where the two main treasures of the nunnery are kept: the Maitreya statue and the Tenjukoku Mandala tapestry.

The Chugu-ji Maitreya image is one of the finest sculptures in Japan, and it is similar to the image in the Koryu-ji temple in Kyoto. Both the Chugu-ji and the Koryu-ji images are of the pensive type of Maitreya which originated in Korea. Carved from one block of camphor wood, the Chugu-ji Maitreya was once colored, but all coloring has long since disappeared. In a seated position, its right foot rests on its upper left leg, its left hand resting on its ankle. Its right hand is poised at its chin as though the image were meditating. Bare from the waist up, its lower body is covered with drapery. A faint smile enlivens its face, and its hair is in two chignons atop its head. Its halo has as decorative elements a lotus flower design with flames and seven small Buddhas with flames about them. It is the loveliest image in the Horyu-ji complex.

The Tenjukoku Mandala (The Heavenly Kingdom of Immortality) commemorates the death of Prince Shotoku at fifty, a devastating blow to his family and a tragedy for the nation. His consort, Tachibana-no-Oiratsume, and her ladies created this embroidered mandala in 622 as a memorial to the prince. Only a portion of the tapestry remains, and it has worked into it an inscription: "The world is folly. Only the Buddha is true." Bright reds and greens and other colors were employed to depict Shotoku in the Buddhist paradise. It is said to have been designed by artists from Korea and then embroidered by the ladies of the princess' court, a tradition which is probably true since the figures in the tapestry are in Korean costumes of the time. Its temples, belfries, bodhisattvas, monks, demons, and phoenixes give a hint of how rich the entire tapestry must have been in its complete form. Today only twelve inches of the tapestry remain.

HORIN-JI

The Horin-ji is a charming, small Buddhist temple from the 600s which is seldom visited by tourists. It is worth the walk of two-thirds of a mile along the road through the fields to the north from the Yumedono to this miniature of the Horyu-ji temple with its very early sculpture.

The Horin-ji was founded by Prince Shotoku's son, Prince Yamashiro-no-Oe in 622 as a place of prayer for the recovery of his father from illness, an illness which led to Shotoku's death in February 622. The temple was no more than a small prayer hall at first, but it was later enlarged into a full-scale temple complex. According to old records, when the Wakakusa-dera (the original Horyu-ji) burned in 670, the monks built three monasteries before deciding on a permanent site for the Horyu-ji. The Horin-ji was one of the three which they built. A violent storm destroyed all of its buildings with the exception of the pagoda in 1645, and the pagoda was hit by lightning in 1940 and it too burned to the ground. All the present buildings are thus reconstructions.

The pagoda of the Horin-ji stands out in the distance as one rounds the bend in a country lane at the hillside cemetery beyond the Horyu-ji. The walled gateway of the Horin-ji opens onto a charming, small temple complex with its three-story pagoda, Shoro (bell tower), Kondo (golden hall), modern Kodo (lecture hall/ treasure hall), and its old shrines. The ground plan of the temple is the same as that of the Horyu-ji so that it provides a miniature reproduction of its more famous neighbor.

PAGODA AND KONDO

The pagoda is a post-1940 replica of the earlier structure, and it originally held a Shaka Nyorai, a Jizo, a Dainichi Nyorai, and the four Shitenno. The Kondo is a 1737 rebuilding of the original golden hall which held a Yakushi Nyorai, a Sho Kannon, a Jizo, a Kichijo-ten, a Bishamon-ten, and a Kokuzo Bodhisattva. All these images are now in the Kodo.

KODO

The Kodo is a fireproof building which serves primarily as the temple treasure hall in which the temple sculptures are today safely preserved. One enters the Kodo from the west side, and the images within are in a row from one end of the hall to the other. They include:

A **Bishamon-ten** of the 800s with his hair piled high on his head and a diadem above his forehead. His belt has a lion mask "stomacher," and his baggy trousers are tucked into boots which come up to his knees. He stands upon two rice bags.

A **Jizo** of the 900–1100s standing on a lotus pedestal with a *centamani* magic jewel in his left hand. Some traces of his original coloring remain.

A **Yakushi Buddha** to whom prayers for Shotoku's recovery would have been made. It is in the same style as the Horyu-ji Shaka triad; it has the same long face and half-smile as in the work of Shiba Tori, even to the frozen folds of the drapery. Its eyes are closed in contemplation.

A **Juichimen Kannon,** an Eleven-Headed Kannon from the 900–1100 era; it has the central position among the images in the Kodo.

A **Kokuzo Bodhisattva** with a stiff and archaic stance and drapery of the same period as the Horyu-ji Shaka triad; it is bare-chested with draperies over its shoulder and forearm hanging to the ground. It holds a small jar by its neck in its left hand.

The **Sho Kannon** holds a lotus blossom on a long stem in its left hand, the blossom topped by a small stupa. The fingers of its right hand form a circle. The large aureole behind it extends for the full length of its body; much of the original color remains on the halo.

Kichijo-ten is the last figure in the row, and it holds a *centamani* jewel in its left hand. Its limbs and pedestal are a later restoration.

Outside the Kodo to the right is the Shoro (bell tower) and to the left the Kuri (priests' quarters). The Myoken-do behind the Kodo has a Myoken image and two attendants.

One can return to the main highway and the bus back to Nara by way of the Hokki-ji temple which was also founded by Shotoku's son. Unfortunately so little remains of its fabric that it can be bypassed. On the left side of the hill while walking toward the Hokki-ji is the Kawara-zuka (Kawara Slope) on which are the ruins of the ancient tile kilns which made roofing tiles for temples of the Nara period. While this is an extended walk to the bus stop, it does provide a very pleasant glimpse of aspects of rural Japan and its rice fields.

The bus back to Nara can be taken either from the Chugu-ji or the Hokki-ji bus stop at the main highway.

APPENDIX

1 Getting to Nara

FROM TOKYO
There are no direct rail links with Nara, but both Osaka and Kyoto have direct rail links with Tokyo, including the fast and efficient *shinkansen* (bullet train). An overnight bus service connects Tokyo with Nara. This is considerably cheaper than the *shinkansen* and is thus an attractive alternative for the budget traveler. Details of schedules can be obtained from either the Tokyo (tel: 03-3502-1461) or Nara Tourist Information Centers.

RAIL ACCESS
Both JR and the Kintetsu Line of the Kinki Nippon Railway offer access by train to Nara.

From Kyoto: The JR line from Kyoto takes one hour; the Kintetsu express takes forty-three minutes at a cheaper fare while the Kintetsu limited express luxury cars make the trip in thirty-three minutes at a surcharge. Both routes leave from Kyoto Central Station.

From Osaka: The JR train takes forty-six minutes from Tennoji Station and an additional fifteen minutes from Osaka Central Station. The Kintetsu express train takes thirty-five minutes from the Namba Station plus an additional fifteen minutes (change at Tsuruhashi Station) if coming from Osaka Central Station; the Kintetsu limited express takes five minutes less from either Osaka station.

BUS TOURS

A number of travel agencies offer bus tours from Kyoto or Osaka to Nara. These tours take one hour each way enroute, and they usually include a luncheon—which leaves far too little time to enjoy the city. One is much better off traveling to Nara by train from either Kyoto or Osaka and then using this guide; much more will be seen at one's own schedule and to suit one's own interests.

LOCAL TRANSPORTATION

Taxis can be hailed on the street or obtained from the taxi rank at the bus station plaza to the rear of the south-west exit of the Kintetsu Nara Station. All sites in this guide book are known to the drivers. Simply state the name of the place you wish to go to, placing equal emphasis on each syllable of the Japanese word (e.g. Daibutsuden = *Dai-bu-tsu-den*). The driver opens and closes passenger doors automatically, so do not attempt to open the door yourself.

A circular bus route reaches the majority of the sites listed in this volume. Bus 1 on the circular route operates in a counter-clockwise direction while bus 2 moves in a clockwise manner. On Bus 1 and 2, as well as bus 63 to the Toshodai-ji and the Yakushi-ji temples, and bus 52 and 60 to the Horyu-ji temple, a recording announces each major stop in English as well as in Japanese. The buses to the Toshodai-ji, the Yakushi-ji, and the Horyu-ji temples each leave from the bus station on Noborioji (to the rear of the south-west exit from the Kintetsu Nara station).

Most buses going outside Nara are boarded from the rear where one takes a numbered ticket from the machine at the door. The ever-changing fare board above the driver indicates the fare to be paid on leaving the bus from the front—the number on your ticket corresponds to the number on the fare board. The ticket and the fare are given to the driver on leaving the bus. Most buses have a change-making machine just behind the driver.

ON FOOT IN NARA

A tourist map to Nara may be obtained from the Tourist Information Centers in Tokyo, Kyoto, Osaka, or Nara—if one wishes to supplement the map in this guidebook. Since streets do not always have name signs, or since the name may appear in Japanese characters and not in English, directions are sometime given in this volume as "turn to the north," etc. If one's sense of direction is fallible, it might be worthwhile to carry a small compass.

NARA TOURIST INFORMATION CENTER

The Tourist Information Center is on Sanjo-dori, one street to the east of the JR station or one street south and one street west from the Kintetsu Nara Station. It is open from 9:00 a.m. to 9:00 p.m. and can provide maps and information. It can also arrange for an English-speaking student guide should one be desired.

APPENDIX
2 Temple and Shrine Information

Some temples charge a small entry fee and some charge an entry fee to specific buildings. Opening times and periods can change without notice and it is best to check with the Nara Tourist Information Center for the latest information.

If a temple's closing day falls on a National Holiday then the temple is usually open that day but closed on the following day.

Name	Hours	Treasure Hall Open
Akishino-dera 秋篠寺 　757 Akishino-cho 　Nara-shi 　Tel: (0742) 45-4600	9:30–16:30	June 6 for Daigensui Myo-o
Byakugo-ji 白毫寺 　392 Byakugoji-cho 　Nara-shi 630 　Tel: (0742) 26-3392	9:00–17:00	All year

Name	*Hours*	*Treasure Hall Open*

Chugu-ji
中宮寺
Horyu-ji
   Ikaruga-machi
   Ikoma-gun
   Nara-ken
   Tel: (0745) 75-2106
	Mar. 21–Sept.30:
	9:00–16:30;
	Oct. 1–
	Mar. 20: 9:00–16:00
	Closed mid-April.
		All year

Daian-ji
大安寺
   2-18-1 Daian-ji
   Nara-shi
   Tel: (0742) 61-6312
	8:00–17:00
	Closed Dec. 25–31.
		Oct. 10–Nov. 10

Daibutsuden
大仏殿
   406-1 Zoshi-cho
   Nara-shi
   Tel: (0742) 22-5511
	Apr.–Sept. 7:30–17:30;
	Oct. 7:30–17:00;
	Nov.–Feb. 8:00–16:30;
	Mar. 8:00–17:00	

Folklore Museum—*see* Minzoku Hakubutsukan

Futai-ji
不退寺
   517 Horen Higashi
   Kakiuchi-cho
   Nara-shi
   Tel: (0742) 22-5278
	8:00–17:00	Nov. 1– 8

Gango-ji—*see* Gokuraku-bo
元興寺

Gokuraku-bo
極楽坊
   11 Chuin-cho
   Nara-shi
   Tel: (0742) 23-1376
	9:00–17:00	All year

Name	*Hours*	*Treasure Hall Open*
Hachiman Shrine 八幡神社 434 Zoshi-cho Nara-shi Tel: (0742) 23-4404	Open daylight hours.	
Hannya-ji 般若寺 221 Hannya-ji-cho Nara-shi Tel: (0742) 22-6287	9:00–17:00	Apr. 29–May 10 Oct. 26–Nov. 10
Heijo-kyu Shiryokan Museum 平城宮跡資料館 2-9-1 Nijo-cho Nara-shi Tel: (0742) 34-3931	Mar.–Oct. 9:00–16:00; Nov.–Feb. 10:00–16:00. Closed Sat. p.m., Sun., Nat. Holidays, New Year holiday.	
Heijo Palace Site 平城宮跡	Open daylight hours. Closed New Year holiday.	
Himuro Shrine 氷室神社 Noborioji-cho Nara-shi 2-min. walk from Nara Nat. Museum	Open daylight hours.	
Hokke-ji 法華寺 Hokke-ji-Naka-machi Nara-shi Tel: (0742) 33-2261	9:00–16:00 Open Sun. & Nat. Holidays.	May 1–15 Oct. 10–Nov. 10

Name	*Hours*	*Treasure Hall Open*
Hokki-ji 法起寺 　1873 Okamoto 　Ikaruga-machi 　Ikoma-gun 　Nara-ken 　Tel: (0745) 75-5559	8:00–16:30	
Horin-ji 法輪寺 　1570 Mitsui 　Ikaruga-machi 　Ikoma-gun 　Nara-ken 　Tel: (0745) 75-2686	Mar.–Nov. 8:00–17:00 Dec.–Feb. 8:00–16:30	All year
Horyu-ji 法隆寺 　878 Horyu-ji 　Ikaruga-machi 　Ikoma-gun 　Nara-ken 　Tel: (0745) 75-2555	Mar. 11–Nov.19: 8:00–16:30; Nov. 20–Mar. 10: 8:00–16:00	All year. Guze Kannon: Apr. 11– May 5, Oct. 22– Nov. 3, in Yume- dono.

Imperial Palace—*see* Heijo Palace Site and Heijo-kyu

Isui-en Garden—*see* Neiraku Museum
依水園

Joruri-ji 浄瑠璃寺（九体寺） 　Kamo-cho Nishio 　Soraku-gun 　Kyoto-fu 　Tel: (0774) 76-2390	Mar.–Nov. 9:00–17:00; Dec.–Feb. 10:00–16:00. Closed National Holidays.	

Name	*Hours*	*Treasure Hall Open*
Jurin-in 十輪院 27 Jurin-in-cho Nara-shi Tel: (0742) 26-6635	9:00–17:00 Closed Aug. 22–23 & New Year holiday.	
Kaidan-in—*see* Todai-ji 戒壇院		
Kasuga Shrine 春日大社 160 Kasugano-cho Nara-shi Tel: (0742) 22-7788	Apr.–Oct. 8:30–16:30 Nov.–Mar. 9:00–16:00	Apr.–Oct. 8:30– 16:30 Nov.–Mar. 9:00– 16:00
Kasuga Wakamiya Shrine 春日若宮神社 Kasugano-cho Nara-shi Tel: (0742) 22-7700	Open daylight hours.	
Kofuku-ji 興福寺 48 Noborioji-cho Nara-shi Tel: (0742) 22-7755	9:00–17:00	All year 9:00–17:00 (Time changes depending on the year.)
Kombu-in 興福院 Horen-cho 88 Nara-shi Tel: (0742) 22-2890	Summer 8:30–16:30 Winter 9:00–16:00	
Minzoku Hakubutsukan 民俗博物館	9:00–17:00. Closed Mondays.	

Name	*Hours*	*Treasure Hall Open*
545 Yata-cho Yamato-Koriyama-shi Nara-ken Tel: (0743) 53-3171	Closed Dec. 28–Jan. 4.	
Nara National Museum 奈良国立博物館 50 Noborioji-cho Nara-shi Tel: (0742) 22-7771	9:00–16:30 Closed Mondays & for exhibit changes. Closed Dec. 26– Jan. 3.	
Nara Prefectural Museum 奈良県立博物館 10-6 Noborioji-cho Nara-shi Tel: (0742) 23-3968	9:00–16:30. Closed holidays, Dec. 28– Jan. 4, & for exhibit changes.	
Nara Rekishi Kyoshitsu 奈良歴史教室 Kintetsu Nara Stn. Bldg., 4–5 Fl. Nara-shi Tel: (0742) 24-3901	10:00–18:00	
Nara Tourist Information Center 23-4 Kami Sanjo-dori Nara-shi Tel: (0742) 22-3900	9:00–21:00	
Neiraku Museum 寧楽美術館 74 Suimon-cho Nara-shi Tel: (0742) 22-2173	10:00–16:30 Closed Tuesdays. Closed Aug. 13–15; Dec. 28–Jan. 4.	

Name	*Hours*	*Treasure Hall Open*

Nigatsu-do—*see* Todai-ji
二月堂

Saidai-ji   8:30–16:30
西大寺
    1-1-5 Shiba-machi
    Saidai-ji
    Nara-shi
    Tel: (0742) 45-4700

Sangatsu-do—*see* Todai-ji
三月堂

Shin-Yakushi-ji   9:00–17:00
新薬師寺
    1352 Takahata
    Fukui-cho
    Nara-shi
    Tel: (0742) 22-3736

Shomu/Komyo Tomb   Open daylight hours.
聖武・光明陵
    Horen Kita-machi
    Nara-shi
    1-chome

Shoso-in   Only open during
正倉院   Oct. 25–Nov. 6.
    Todai-ji compound
    Tel: (0742) 26-2811

Tamukeyama
Hachiman-gu—*see* Hachiman Shrine
手向山八幡宮

Name	*Hours*	*Treasure Hall Open*

Todai-ji
東大寺
   406-1 Zoshi-cho
   Tel: (0742) 22-5511
	Apr.–Sept. 7:30–17:30;
	Oct. 7:30–17:00;
	Nov.–Feb. 8:00–16:30;
	Mar. 8:00–17:00.	

Toshodai-ji
唐招提寺
   13-46 Gojo-cho
   Nara-shi
   Tel: (0742) 33-7900
	8:30–16:30	Mar. 21–May 19;
		Sept. 15–Nov. 3.

Yakushi-ji
薬師寺
   457 Nishi-no-kyo-
   machi
   Nara-shi
   Tel: (0742) 33-6001
	8:30–17:00	Oct. 20–Nov. 10

Yamato Bunkakan
大和文化館
   1-11-6 Gakuen
   Minami
   Nara-shi
   Tel: (0742) 45-0544
	10:00–16:00
	Closed Mondays.	

Zuto 頭塔 Kami-Shimizu-cho	Visible behind its fence. View by appointment—inquire at Nara Tourist Info. Center.	

APPENDIX
3 Festival Calendar

January

1–3   **Hatsu-mode** New Year Celebration. January 1 is a national holiday when all public buildings are closed. The new year is rung in at midnight on December 31 when the bells of Buddhist temples are rung 108 times to signify the 108 shortcomings of mankind—and to absolve believers of past errors for a fresh start in the new year. Hatsu-mode is the first visit of the year to temples or shrines to pray for a good year.

1   **Fire Brigade Ceremony** at Sarusawa Pond. The annual Fire Brigade Review with fire drills and the playing of hoses into the air.

1–10   **Yakushi-ji's treasure hall** open.

1–15   Viewing of **Kichijo-ten image** at Joruri-ji.

5   **Hatsu Ebisu** (first Ebisu celebration) at Minami-ichi-cho, near Sarusawa Pond. A festival honoring Ebisu, the Shinto deity of good luck. Stalls selling good-luck charms line the street.

8 (monthly)   **Turning of the Sutras** at Yakushi-ji Kodo. A ceremony on the **eighth of each month** throughout the year.

15   **Adults' Day** (a national holiday). A day celebrating young people who have come of age and may now vote.

15   **Yamayaki** (Grass Burning Ceremony) at Mt. Wakakusa. At 6:00 p.m. conch shells are blown.

23   **Sasazaki Festival** at Daian-ji. A commemoration of the accession of Emperor Konin, the last emperor to reign for a full era in Nara in the late 700s. Saké is warmed in bamboo stalks and offered to all present after a memorial rite. It is a crowded festival since this commemorative saké is said to prevent cancer.

February

2–3   **Setsubun.** The equinox celebration which marks the end of winter under the lunar calendar—a time to bring in good luck by driving out evil and demons by the throwing of beans. The ceremony takes place at most temples. At 7:00 p.m., after a skit, Bishamon-ten chases demons around the To-Kondo of the Kofuku-ji temple. A similar event is held at the Horyu-ji Saien-do.

3   **Saito Goma-e** at Gango-ji/Gokuraku-bo. A fire-walking ceremony where faith keeps the participants from being burned.

3   **Mandoro Lantern Lighting Ceremony** at Kasuga Shrine. The 3,000 lanterns of the Kasuga Shrine are lit at 6:00 p.m. to welcome spring. Bugaku performance by torchlight at 8:00 p.m.

11   **National Foundation Day** (a national holiday).

March

1–14   **Shuni-e Ceremony** at the Todai-ji Nigatsudo. Another "end of winter" celebration. From March 12–14, at 8:00 p.m., the temple priests parade with 21-foot-long flaming torches and scatter the embers over the crowds below. The embers burn out sins and bring good luck.

12, 13, 14, 15   Omizutori at Todai-ji Nigatsudo. Sacred water is drawn from the temple well by priests after a vigorous Tartar dance brandishing a five-foot-long torch over the water to purify it. The water is distributed to those in attendance as a good luck charm. (A very crowded time when lodging and food are difficult to obtain.)

13   **Saru Matsuri** at Kasuga Shrine. A re-enactment of a ceremony begun in 850 when the imperial messenger was welcomed to the shrine. Costumes of the ninth century are worn. The

March *(cont'd)*

ceremonies consist of: arrival of the imperial messenger, purification of the imperial messenger, offerings to the kami by the imperial messenger, ceremony of offerings by Shinto priests, procession of the sacred white horse, and Yamato-mai ceremonial dances by the priests in robes of black, white, and red at the inner shrine to please the shrine kami. 9 a.m.

15   **Rice Planting Festival** at Kasuga Shrine. As a prayer for a good harvest, *miko* (shrine maidens) do a dance imitative of the planting of rice plants. 10 a.m.

Mid-March   **Opening of the Kyudo** at Daian-ji. The Octagonal Hall is open to the public to reveal the image of Bato Kannon.

Mid-March to **Mid-April**   Apricot blossom time.

20 or 21   **Spring Equinox Day.** A national holiday.

20–April 7   **Komyo Kannon image** on view at Hokke-ji.

20–May 19   **Toshodai-ji treasure hall** open.

21–May 20   **Kichijo-ten image** on view at Joruri-ji.

23–26   **Memorial services** for the soul of Prince Shotoku in the Sangyo-in, Horyu-ji.

30–April 5   **Hana-e Shiki** (Flower Offering Rite). The Yakushi-ji Kondo is decorated with ten kinds of artificial flowers as offerings to Yakushi, a ceremony dating to a service held by the Emperor Horikawa in the late eleventh century for the recovery of his consort from illness. Her attendants then decorated the Kondo as part of the ceremony. On the evening of the last day, a red, a blue, and a black demon, each carrying torches, are finally driven from the Kondo by Bishamon-ten.

April

Early to **mid-April**   Cherry blossom time in Nara Park.

1–7   **Hina-e Shiki** at Hokke-ji. Thirty images of Zenzaidoji (youthful aides to Fudo), donated by devotees, are displayed before the Hondo.

5   **O-taimatsu** (Fire Festival) at Shin Yakushi, 7:00 p.m. Twelve priests representing the Twelve Divine Generals carry torches to drive three demons in red, blue, and black from the Kondo. Prayers are addressed to Yakushi for the cure of illnesses.

8   **Hana Matsuri** (Flower Festival) for the Buddha's Birthday at

Todai-ji and other temples. The Buddha's birthday is celebrated with flowers and by the pouring of sweet tea over an image of the newborn Buddha, the image being placed in a temporary "flower temple." At some temples there is a procession of young children in traditional garb.

8　**Tsuro-no-hocho** at Kasuga Shrine. A demonstration of traditional court cooking by a master chef of the Shijo School. Bugaku dances afterwards.

11–May 5　**Guze Kannon** on view in Horyu-ji Yumedono.

Mid-April　Chugu-ji Festival.

Second Saturday and **Sunday**　Ochamori at Saidai-ji. A mirthful tea drinking ceremony in honor of the priest Eison who restored the Saidai-ji in the 1200s. A huge tea whisk is used to mix *matcha* (powdered green tea) in a gigantic tea bowl which is then drunk by participants. From 9:00 a.m. to 4:00 p.m.

Second Sunday　Tsubaki Matsuri at Byakugo-ji. 10 a.m.

29　**Conservation Day**. A national holiday.

29–May 10　**Hannya-ji treasure hall** open.

May

1–15　**Spring opening** of the inner grounds at Hokke-ji. Komyo Kannon on view.

1–15　**Daigensui Myo-o** on view at Akishino-dera.

2　**Shomu Tenno Sai.** Emperor Shomu Commemorative Service at Todai-ji. A commemoration of the death of the Emperor Shomu. The dancing *Nembutsu* is performed by priests, and a parade in eighth-century costumes takes place. 1 p.m.

3　**Constitution Day.** A national holiday.

5　**Gagaku Concert** and **Bugaku** performance in Manyo Gardens from 1:00 p.m. to 4:00 p.m.

5　**Children's Day** (formerly "Boys' Day"). A national holiday.

11–12　**Ceremonial Dances** at Kasuga Shrine. The Okina and Sanbaso dances in the afternoon are a prelude to the Takigi Noh at Kofuku-ji.

11–12　**Takigi Noh** at Kofuku-ji. Performance of Noh plays by four schools of Noh at the site of the former Nandai-mon gate. Performance begins at 4:00 p.m., and at dusk the plays are illuminated by torches and bonfires.

May *(cont'd)*

Mid-May Blooming of the famous wisteria vine at Kasuga Shrine.

19   **Uchiwamaki** (Fan Throwing Ceremony) at Toshodai-ji. A festival in honor of the priest Kakusei who helped to reconstruct the Toshodai-ji in the Kamakura period (1185–1333). Heart-shaped fans are thrown by priests to onlookers. These are good-luck charms which scare away evil spirits. 4 p.m.

June

5–7   **Kaisan-ki.** A memorial service for the priest Ganjin at Toshodai-ji. The doors to the Kaisan-do (Founder's Hall) are open so that the lovely statue of Ganjin may be seen. From 9 a.m.

6–8   **Komyo Kannon** on view at Hokke-ji.

17   **Saikusa Matsuri** (Ceremony of the Lily) at Isagawa Shrine (south of the Tourist Information Office). An offering to the shrine kami of lilies from sacred Mt. Miwa (outside Sakurai) and of saké in a cask decorated with lilies. Four *miko* (shrine maidens) do a dance while holding the flowers—a ceremony to ward off illnesses. 10:30 a.m.

23   **Také Kuyo** at Daian-ji. 1 p.m.

July

23–24   **Jizo-bon**   Ceremony at Fukuchi-in (5 p.m.) and **Jizo-e** Ceremony at other temples. A ceremony in honor of the Bodhisattva Jizo who is the patron of children and pregnant women.

August

2   **Viewing of the founder's image** at Todai-ji. The annual showing of the image of the priest Roben in the Kaisan-do of the Todai-ji on the anniversary of his birth.

7   **Ominugui** in the Todai-ji Daibutsuden. An annual ceremonial cleaning of the Great Buddha image. 7 a.m.

14–15   **Mandoro Ceremony** at Kasuga Shrine. The lighting of the 3,000 lanterns of the shrine at 7:00 p.m.—a repeat of the February 3 festival.

15   **Daimonji Okuribi** on Mt. Takamado. A lighting of a fire in the

form of the character *Dai* (great) to light the spirit of the dead back to the other world at the end of the Obon period. ("Great" here refers to the Buddhist Law.) This ceremony was begun after World War II to console the spirits of the wartime military dead. 6 p.m. ceremony; 8 p.m. lighting.

September

Mid-September (night of the full moon)   Uneme Ceremony at Sarusawa Pond. A parade of priests in purple and girls with white veils who bring flowers to the legendary willow tree at which Uneme left her clothes before drowning in the pond. In the evening, musicians in a dragon-shaped boat cast a great fan of flowers on the waters of the pond to console Uneme's spirit. From 4:30 p.m.

Sanbutsu Kangetsu-e at Toshodai-ji. In the evening, tea is served to the statue of Ganjin in the Kaisan-do and candles are offered to the three main images in the Hondo. 6 p.m.

15   Day of Respect for the Elderly. A national holiday.

15 to **November 3   Toshodai-ji treasure hall** open.

23 or **24   Autumn Equinox Day**. A national holiday. On this day Buddhist temples hold services in memory of family ancestors.

October

10   Health and Sports Day. A national holiday.

10–November 10   Opening of inner grounds at Hokke-ji.

Mid-October to **early November** on Sundays and National Holidays
Shika no Tsunokiri in the deer pen (Rokuen) in the Kasuga Shrine Park. The annual de-horning of bucks who are lassoed in the deer pen and then have their horns sawed off. 10 a.m.

10 to **November 10   Daian-ji treasure hall** open.

Second Sunday   Ochamori Ceremony at Saidai-ji. See the April listing for a description of this ceremony. 9 a.m.

19–26   Shaka Nembutsu at Toshodai-ji. A service in honor of Amida Buddha.

End October to **early November   Yakushi-ji treasure hall** open.

22 to **November 3** Viewing of the **Guze Kannon** at Horyu-ji Yumedono.

25 to **November 6   Shoso-in grounds** open.

November *(cont'd)*

25 to **November 8**   The annual showing of a portion of the **Emperor Shomu's treasures** from the Shoso-in are on view at the Nara National Museum new building.

25 to **November 8**   **Komyo Kannon** on view at Hokke-ji.

26–November 10   **Hannya-ji treasure hall** open.

November

Chrysanthemum displays at temples and shrines.

1–30   **Kichijo-ten image** on view at Joruri-ji.

3   **Culture Day.** A national holiday. **Bugaku** and **Gagaku Performances** at Manyo Gardens and the Kasuga Shrine. The Gagaku concert at the Kasuga inner shrine is at 10:00 a.m. Bugaku at the Manyo Gardens is from 1:00 p.m. to 4:00 p.m.

23   **Labor Thanksgiving Day.** A national holiday.

December

16   **Shikkongo-shin image** on view at Sangatsu-do.

16–18   **Kasuga Wakamiya On-matsuri.** An annual festival when prayers are made for a good harvest and for protection against evil. On the sixteenth, prayers are offered to the kami of the shrine and Kagura dances are performed. At midnight the kami is moved to the O-Tabisho, a temporary rustic shrine. On the seventeenth, a procession in ancient costume, accompanied by classical music, parades at 1:00 p.m. from the Kofuku-ji to the shrine. In the evening, Kagura, Dengaku, and Sarugaku dances and Bugaku are performed. On the eighteenth, Noh and sumo are offered to the kami before the spirit is returned from the O-Taibisho to the main shrine.

23   **Emperor's Birthday.** A national holiday.

Late December   **Ominugui** at Yakushi-ji. A ceremonial cleaning of the Buddhist images in the Kondo. 1 p.m.